Blue Tide Rising

A memoir of the
Union Army in
North Carolina

by

Major General Jacob D. Cox

edited by Jack E. Fryar, Jr.

Dram Tree
Books

First Edition 1900
Published in the United States of America by Dram Tree Books.

Publisher's Cataloging-in-Publication Data
(Provided by DRT Press)

Cox, Jacob D. (Jacob Dolson), 1828-1900.
    Blue tide rising : a memoir of the Union army in North Carolina / by Major General Jacob D. Cox ; edited by Jack Fryar, Jr.
    p. cm.
    Include bibliographical references.
    ISBN 978-0-9786248-3-5
1. Cox, Jacob D. (Jacob Dolson), 1828-1900. 2. North Carolina--History--Civil War, 1861-1865--Personal narratives. 3. United States--History--Civil War, 1861-1865--Personal narratives. I. Fryar, Jack E. II. Title.

E477.7 .C69 2007
973.7320--dc22

10 9 8 7 6 5 4 3 2 1

Volume discounts available.
Call or e-mail for terms.

Dram Tree Books
P.O. Box 7183
Wilmington, N.C. 28406
(910) 538-4076
www.dramtreebooks.com
Potential authors: visit our website or email us for submission guidelines

Contents

Kinston—Enemy attack our left front—Rout of Upham's brigade—Main line firm—Ruger's division reaches the field—Enemy repulsed—End of first day's fight—Extending our trenches on the left—Sharp skirmishing of the 9th—Bragg's reinforcements—His attack of the both—Final repulse and retreat of the enemy.

CHAPTER XLVIII....47

JUNCTION WITH SHERMAN AT GOLDSBOROUGH—THE MARCH ON RALEIGH—CESSATION OF HOSTILITIES

Occupation of Kinston—Opening of Neuse River—Rebel ram destroyed—Listening to the distant battle at Bentonville—Entering Goldsborough—Meeting Sherman—Grant's congratulations—His own plans—Sketch of Sherman's march—Lee and Johnston's correspondence—Their gloomy outlook—Am made commandant of Twenty-third Corps—Terry assigned to Tenth—Schofield promoted in the Regular Army—Stanton's proviso—Ill effects of living on the country—Stopping it in North Carolina—Camp jubilee over the fall of Richmond—Changes in Sherman's plans—Our march on Smithfield—House-burning—News of Lee's surrender—Overtures from Governor Vance—Entering Raleigh—A mocking-bird's greeting—Further negotiations as to North Carolina—Johnston proposes an armistice—Broader scope of negotiations—The Southern people desire peace—Terrors of non-combatants assuaged—News of Lincoln's assassination—Precautions to preserve order—The dawn of peace.

CHAPTER XLIX....67

THE SHERMAN-JOHNSTON CONVENTION

Sherman's earlier views of the slavery question—Opinions in 1864—War rights vs. statesmanship—Correspondence with Halleck—Conference with Stanton at Savannah—Letter to General Robert Anderson—Conference with Lincoln at City Point—First effect of the assassination of the President—Situation on the Confederate side—Davis at Danville—Cut off from Lee—Goes to Greensborough—Calls Johnston to conference—Lee's surrender—The Greensborough meeting—Approach of Stoneman's cavalry raid—Vance's deputation to Sherman—Davis orders their arrest—Vance asserts his loyalty—Attempts to concentrate Confederate forces on the Greensborough-Charlotte line—Cabinet meeting—Overthrow of the Confederacy acknowledged—Davis still hopeful—Yields to the cabinet—Dictates Johnston's letter to Sherman—Sherman's reply—Meeting arranged—Sherman sends preliminary correspondence to Washington—The Durham meeting—The negotiations—Two

CHAPTER L....87

THE SECOND SHERMAN—JOHNSTON CONVENTION—SURRENDER

CHAPTER LI....109

PAROLING AND DISBANDING JOHNSTON'S ARMY—CLOSING SCENES OF THE WAR IN NORTH CAROLINA

Union men—Elements of new strife—The negroes—Household service—Wise dealing with the labor question—No money—Death of manufactures—Necessity the mother of invention—Uses of adversity—Peace welcomed—Visit to Greene's battlefield at Guilford-Old-Court-House.

Editors Note

In the war that took more American lives than any before or since, North Carolina was a reluctant participant. The state was one of the last to withdraw from the Union in 1861, but when it did, it stepped up and honored its commitment to the Confederacy like no other. More North Carolina men and boys marched away from their homes and loved ones to carry the banner of the Confederate States of America than any other, and more Tar Heels left heir blood, limbs and lives on Civil War battlefields than any other.

By 1862 the Union had reclaimed at least part of North Carolina, when General Ambrose Burnside's troops re-occupied the Outer Banks, New Bern, and a substantial portion of the Albemarle. But south of them, soldiers wearing the gray and butternut of the Confederate army still controlled the state. This was especially true in the southernmost portion of North Carolina, where Wilmington had become the most important port in the Confederacy. Because the city – the largest in the state at the time – was too far inland to be shelled from the sea, the only way to take it would be by assaulting overland or up the Cape Fear River. To prevent this, the Confederates built eleven major forts and installations to guard the port. The largest of these, Fort Fisher, had walls that stretched for more than a mile on the southern tip of New Hanover County. The earthen and sand fortification was the largest in the South, and its imposing size and design compared favorably with the great forts of Europe.

Union war planners were content to put off tackling Wilmington and the forts that guarded it until easier prizes had been plucked. But by late 1864, Wilmington had become the last source of the supplies so desperately needed by Robert E. Lee's Army of Northern Virginia, who were fighting a desperate fight against Grant's army around Fredericksburg. The well-loved commander of the South's armies plainly stated that if Wilmington fell, he could not keep his army in the field. For Union commanders, the time had come to take Wilmington.

The first attempt to do that came on Christmas Eve 1864, when the largest fleet of American warships ever assembled gathered off the North Carolina coast at Fort Fisher. It was a botched attempt that resulted in a humiliating defeat for the Union. But two weeks later the fleet was back. The largest naval bombardment in history – over 19,000 shells – softened up the beleaguered Confederates under Col. William Lamb, while Union soldiers under General Alfred H. Terry landed for the assault. When the land attack came, it was a vicious fight, tooth-and-nail fight that saw thousands die on the sandy beaches beside New Inlet. But when it was all over, Union forces had the toehold they needed to take Wilmington and end North Carolina's participation in the war.

Ohioan Jacob Dolson Cox was busy leading his men in the fight in Tennessee when the Battles of Fort Fisher occurred. He missed the bloodshed that would signal the beginning of the end of the Confederacy. But immediately after the fort was in Union hands, his division received orders to head for North Carolina. In a remarkable feat of movement, he and his men quickly arrived at Fort Fisher. From there, he would participate in the fight to take Fort Anderson and Wilmington. Then he and his men joined the march through North Carolina, participating in or witnessing every major battle fought in the state through the end of the war. His memoirs, originally published in 1900 (the year of his death), provide remarkable behind-the scenes insight into not just the fighting that went on, but also into the character of the men who acted out the last scenes in America's bloodiest drama in North Carolina. This book excerpts the chapters dealing with the closing acts of the war in the Tar Heel State. It is a telling narrative of determination, desperation, honor and courage on both sides of the issue. As such, Cox's memoir brings the people who fought the war to life, and conveys lessons about duty, honor and courage that have merit even today.

Jack E. Fryar, Jr.
Wilmington, N.C.
June 2007

Major General Jacob Dolson Cox

CHAPTER XLVI

CAMPAIGN IN NORTH CAROLINA—CAPTURE OF WILMINGTON

Rendezvous at Washington—Capture of Fort Fisher—Schofield ordered to North Carolina—Grant and Schofield visit Terry—Department of North Carolina—Army of the Ohio in the field—Correspondence of Grant and Sherman—Sherman conscious of his risks but hopeful of great results—His plan of march from Savannah—Relation of Wilmington to New Berne—Our arrival at Washington—The Potomac frozen—Peace conference at Fort Monroe—Interview with Mr. Stanton—The thirteenth amendment of the Constitution—Political excitement at the capital—A little dinner-party—Garfield, H. W. Davis, and Schenck—Davis on Lincoln—Destination of our army—Embarkation—Steamship "Atlantic"—Visit to Fort Monroe—The sea-voyage—Cape Fear Inlet—General Terry's lines—Bragg the Confederate commander—Reconnoitering his lines—The colored troops—"Monitor" engaged with Fort Anderson—Alternate plans—Marching on Wilmington by the west bank of the river—My column opposite the town—Orders not applicable to the situation—Difficulty of communication—Use of discretion—Wilmington evacuated—A happy result.

O n Thursday the 26th of January, 1865, I received a telegram from General Schofield directing me to join my command without delay, and I started from my home in northern Ohio the same evening.[1] I had spent a week in a delightful visit with my family after two years of absence from them, and had been rapidly improving in health. The growing faith that the campaign of the winter and spring would end in complete victory for the national arms created an ardent zeal to be about it and to have an active hand in the final scenes. Our orders had indicated Annapolis as our port of rendezvous, and our destination the Army of the Potomac in front of Petersburg.[2] On reaching Annapolis Junction in the night of the 28th, I learned that my division was in Washington, and followed it, arriving there in the morning of the 29th.[3]

The change from Annapolis to Washington and Alexandria had been made by Grant upon a suggestion of General Halleck that there was no shelter at Annapolis for such a body of troops, whilst there was enough at the capital. As the winter weather was then severe, this thoughtfulness saved the command much suffering.[4] The military situation had also changed materially by the capture of Fort Fisher on the North Carolina coast, on the very day we embarked on the transports at Clifton (January 15th). This capture by the forces under General A. H. Terry was one step in the preparation of a new base for Sherman in his march northward through the Carolinas, and Grant was most anxious that it should be followed by the occupation of Wilmington. His desire to strengthen his own army was made secondary to his determination to make Sherman's movement an assured success. He wrote to Sherman on the 21st that he would send Schofield to Wilmington, if, as was rumored, the fall of that place had followed the capture of Fort Fisher.[5] On the 24th he had made up his mind to send Schofield there anyhow, and was going himself to inspect the fort and the situation at the mouth of Cape Fear River. He telegraphed for Schofield to join him on this visit to Terry, and the outline of the new campaign was then arranged. A new department of North Carolina was decided upon, Schofield was to command it, his army in the field to consist of two provisional corps besides the Twenty-third, of which Terry was to command one, and the other for a time fell to me. This field force was to retain our old title of the Army of the Ohio. On Schofield's recommendation the brevet rank of major-general was given to General Ruger, and that of brigadier to Colonel Henderson of the One Hundred and Twelfth Illinois, for services at Franklin.[6] Sherman had heard of the fall of Fort Fisher before he broke his

General Ulysses S. Grant (above) and MajGen. Henry Halleck (below)

communications with Savannah, and was assured of a new base there, even if the line from New Berne to Goldsborough should not be opened.

The correspondence between Sherman and Grant at this time is very characteristic of both men, and throws a bright light on their unselfish friendship and their earnest purpose to bring the war to a successful end without rest or delay. In his letter of the 21st of January, after giving the latest details of his situation, Sherman adds: "I am told that Congress meditates a bill to make another lieutenant-general for me. I have written to John Sherman to stop it if it is designed for me.[7] It would be mischievous, for there are enough rascals who would try to sow differences between us, whereas you and I now are in perfect understanding. I would rather have you in command than anybody else, for you are fair, honest, and have at heart the same purpose that should animate all. I should emphatically decline any commission calculated to bring us into rivalry, and I ask you to advise all your friends in Congress to this effect, especially Mr. Washburne. I doubt if men in Congress fully realize that you and I are honest in our professions of want of ambition. I know that I feel none, and to-day will gladly surrender my position and influence to any other who is better able to wield the power. The flurry attending my recent success will soon blow over and give place to new developments."[8]

Replying on the 1st of February, Grant said: "I have received your very kind letter, in which you say you would decline, or are opposed to, promotion. No one would be more pleased at your advancement than I, and if you should be placed in my position and I put

General John M. Schofield

subordinate, it would not change our relations in the least. I would make the same exertions to support you that you have ever done to support me, and I would do all in my power to make our cause win."[9]

That Sherman knew his campaign in the Carolinas would involve great risks, and had no blind confidence in his fortune, was shown by his reply to the well-known letter of congratulation which President Lincoln sent him upon the surrender of Savannah:[10] "The motto 'Nothing venture, nothing win,' which you refer to, is most appropriate, and should I venture too much and happen to lose, I shall bespeak your charitable inference."[11]

In writing to Grant also, on the 29th of January, in a very full and interesting letter, he said: "I expect Davis will move Heaven and earth to catch me, for success to my column is fatal to his dream of empire. Richmond is not more vital to his cause than Columbia and the heart of South Carolina."[12]

The general plan which he adopted was to threaten both Charleston and Augusta with the wings of his army, keeping the enemy in doubt as to his purpose as long as possible, whilst he pushed his centre rapidly toward Columbia. He had no mind to waste time in serious operations against Charleston, for he knew that it must fall when his advance threatened to cut it off from communication with Richmond. From Columbia he planned to march on Raleigh by way of Goldsborough, the last-named place being connected by railroad with both Wilmington and New Berne, and being therefore the objective

Secretary of War Stanton

of General Schofield's movements from both seaports. Beaufort, the harbor of New Berne, was deeper than the mouth of Cape Fear River, and was therefore to be made the principal base of supply for Sherman when he should enter North Carolina; but Wilmington was so much further south that prudence required it to be first occupied and provisioned to give Sherman temporary supply, if any contingency should make it necessary to him before the railroad from New Berne to Goldsborough could be rebuilt. These subsidiary operations in North Carolina were to be our special task.[13]

On reaching Washington, I found that my troops were just arriving on trains from the West. They were temporarily placed in barracks in the city, till the fleet of transports should be ready. The unusual severity of the winter had frozen the Potomac, and Annapolis was also blocked with ice, so that the quartermaster's department had to wait two or three days for a change of weather, before fixing the point of departure.[14] The time passed pleasantly for me, since it gave me the opportunity of renewing old acquaintance with public men, and of observing for myself the spirit which animated political circles at the capital. Mr. Lincoln with Mr. Seward had gone to Fort Monroe to meet Mr. Stephens and others, commissioned by the Richmond government to confer informally as to the possibilities of peace. The Confederate officials were at Grant's headquarters on the 1st of February, "very desirous of going to Washington to see Mr. Lincoln," as the General-in-Chief wrote Sherman incidentally. From his interview with them, Grant was convinced that "the peace feeling within the rebel lines is gaining ground rapidly," but he added, "This, however, should not relax our energies in the least, but should stimulate us to greater activity."[15]

Going to pay my respects to Secretary Stanton at the War Department, I was met by him in an exceedingly cordial way, and in parting, after an interesting visit, he congratulated me on my promotion, saying I owed nobody any thanks for it, as it had been fully and fairly won. I owe it to him to mention this, for so much was current about the brusqueness of his intercourse with army officers, that he is entitled to the testimony that, on this as on all other occasions when I met him personally, nothing could be kinder or more considerate than his manner to me.

My visit to Washington happened to include the day on which the constitutional amendment abolishing slavery passed the House. Breakfasting with Chief-Justice Chase, I met also Henry Ward Beecher, and the great historical event was, of course, the central subject of conversation. The forecast by such men of the effect upon the country and upon the world made a blending of solid wisdom with brilliant eloquence not to be forgotten. My friend Governor Dennison was Postmaster-General, and in his house I had full opportunity to judge of the keen, almost feverish interest with which public men and leading citizens were following the rapid march of both military and civil affairs. Coming, as I was, out of the rough winter campaign of the West for a brief halt in the

Henry Ward Beecher

centre of political activity, before sailing to the swamp-lined shores of Carolina, there was something almost unreal, though fascinating, in the contrast of the excitement of the field with the totally different but scarcely less absorbing excitement which I saw in every face.

Garfield arranged a little dinner at which, besides himself, I met General Schenck and Henry Winter Davis, all of them playing leading roles in the House of Representatives. We four were alone, and it was a rare opportunity for me to hear unrestrained discussion of everything in public affairs. Nearly every phase of current political and military events was treated in brilliant and trenchant criticism, and the conversation turned at last upon the peace conference going on at Fort Monroe. Mr. Davis was a Marylander, who was second to none in uncompromising loyalty to the Union, and had an acknowledged pre-eminence in eloquent advocacy of the National cause. He, however, did not understand or appreciate Mr. Lincoln, and in the celebrated "Wade and Davis manifesto" of the previous year, had opposed the re-election of the President. He now let loose in a witty and scathing denunciation of Lincoln and all his works. The current epithets among the President's opponents, of which "baboon" was one of the mildest, were flung at him with a venom that, to me, was half shocking and half comical. The soldier habit of making the Hurrah for Lincoln our answering war-cry to the Hurrah for Davis of our enemies in the field, made a bewildering puzzle of such an outburst. The meeting with the Southern commissioners was denounced as a weak compromising of our cause. He saw no force in the argument that weak hearts among us would be strengthened when they saw that now as upon former overtures the Confederate authorities insisted upon independence as the necessary condition of peace, whilst Mr. Lincoln stood firmly for restoration of the Union and abolition of slavery as the essentials. The curious fact was that such a man, ably busied for four years in political co-operation with the President, living in the same city, in frequent personal contact with him, had utterly failed to measure his character and his intellect, or to get even a glimmering idea of what lay beneath that ungraceful exterior and that quaint and humorous speech. The elegant orator and polished man of the world felt no magnetism but that of repulsion; and his senses were so dulled by it that he never guessed the wisdom and the breadth, the subtle policy and the deep statesmanship, the luminous insight and the unfaltering purpose which now seem writ so plain in Lincoln's words and deeds.

General Schenck did not appear to differ greatly from Davis, but what he said was in short, trenchant sentences, interjected from time to time. Garfield treated the outburst as a sort of extravaganza, and in his position as host did not seriously debate, but rallied his friend with good-humored persiflage, met his outbursts with jovial laughter and prodded him to fresh explosions by shafts of wit. It was a strange and not altogether exhilarating experience for me; but I had afterward to learn that the belittling view of Lincoln was the common one among public men in Washington. The people at a distance got a juster perspective, and knowing him by his written papers and his public acts, divined him better and gave him a loyal support hardly to be distinguished from their devotion to the cause of the country itself. We may fairly conclude that the failure of so many men near the President to understand him is not creditable to their sagacity; but we must also admit that a first impression and a superficial view would in his case be almost surely misleading, and that to correct it would take better opportunities for an intimate study of the man than most public men would have, and most would not care to seek them. The belittling view of men in power fits best our self-esteem.

As soon as General Schofield got back from his trip to Fort Fisher with

Grant, he had issued his orders for our movement which was to take place as soon as the ice would permit our transports to enter or leave the harbors on Chesapeake Bay and the Potomac. My own division was to take the lead and sail to Cape Fear River. Couch's would come next and land at Beaufort for operations on the New Berne line. Ruger's (the new troops) would sail last, and find orders at Fort Monroe in going down the bay, deciding whether its destination should be Wilmington or Beaufort.[16] Meagher's provisional division of detachments belonging to Sherman's army was temporarily attached to us, for it was too late to join Sherman by way of Savannah. Meagher had ordered it to rendezvous at New York, but Grant changed its destination to Washington with the purpose just stated. Its commander had gone on to New York in advance without any understanding with army headquarters, and the convivial and unsystematic Irishman thereby fell into trouble.[17]

On Thursday the 2d of February, General Schofield was able to issue his final orders for embarkation. Only vessels enough for two brigades of my division had been able to reach Alexandria, and Casement's brigade was sent by rail to Annapolis to take ship there and to be followed immediately by Meagher's provisional command.[18] Friday was spent in getting troops on board the ships at Annapolis and systematizing their accommodation for the voyage. One of our transports was the "Atlantic," Captain Gray, which, as the crack ship of the Collins Line of New York and Liverpool packets, had led the van of the ocean greyhounds in the days of wooden hulls and side-wheels. General Schofield and myself made our headquarters on this ship. On each of the other vessels the senior officer was made responsible for all the troops on board, and was confidentially authorized, after it should enter Chesapeake Bay, to instruct the master of the ship to make the best of his way to Cape Fear Inlet as the rendezvous for the division.[19] General Grant had asked the War Department to arrange for a patrol of the coast by the navy during the transit of Schofield's little army.[20]

On Saturday the 4th we had expected to start at daybreak, but a heavy fog delayed us. When it lifted, we made our way slowly down the Potomac, the drifting ice obstructing the passage so that we could only go at a snail's pace, backing and filling to keep in the ice openings and to save injury to the vessel. Starting at ten o'clock, we only reached the head of Kettlebottom Shoals by nightfall of the short winter day, making less than twenty miles. The passage of the shoals was too dangerous for so large a vessel in the dark, and we dropped anchor for the night. I had made it my first task on Friday evening to have a complete understanding with Captain Gray, and to get his suggestions as to the orders I desired to issue for the conduct and discipline of the troops while on board ship for which I was responsible. He was a gentleman of ability and large experience in his profession, and co-operated with me so cordially that our week on board the "Atlantic" was a most comfortable one, full of interest and enjoyment, though we met rough weather outside the capes. My order was issued on Saturday and rigidly enforced during the voyage. By Captain Gray's invitation I made my office in his chart-room on the upper deck, enforcing regular tours of duty for officers and men of the division, of whom nearly 2000 were on board. In the intervals, when the captain was not himself on the bridge, we exchanged stories of our very different experiences, and I found his conversation both interesting and instructive. We had besides, of course, the large circle of comrades and old friends in the cabin, and for those who escaped sea-sickness the hours never hung heavy.[21]

Weighing anchor at daybreak on Sunday morning, we passed Kettle Bottom Shoals safely, and found much more open water in the lower river. The day was mild and calm, and we made good progress to Fort Monroe, where we stopped in the evening to take on board a supply of ammunition. While this work was going on, I took advantage of the opportunity to land in a small boat and pass through the place by moonlight. As one of the largest and most important of the fortresses of the old style, with heavy walls of masonry, casemated, and with regular moat, it was an interesting study to a soldier, and all the more so as we were then in the full heat of the discussion of the relative value of such formal works compared with mere earthworks, of which Fort Fisher, to which we were bound, was a very striking example. It was admitted that modern ordnance could soon knock the walls into a rubbish-heap, but Fort Sumter had raised the supplementary debate, whether the rubbish-heap did not begin a new chapter in the defence, longer and more important than the first period of attack.

As soon as the ammunition was on board and properly stowed, our voyage was resumed, and at daybreak we had passed out of Chesapeake Bay, joining our consorts of the transport fleet near Cape Henry, and were running

Fort Monroe in Virginia.

Fort Fisher's mile-long sea face as it appeared before the fort's fall.

down the coast along the even line of keys which lie as a breastwork against the Atlantic Ocean outside of the much indented coast proper of North Carolina. The wind was moderate and off shore, so that Captain Gray laid his course straight for Cape Hatteras, with only offing enough to keep in a good depth of water,— say fifteen or twenty miles. At intervals during the day we could see isolated clumps of pine-trees rising out of the water, like low-lying, blue clouds, so that we could hardly say that we were wholly out of sight of land. We passed Cape Hatteras late in the afternoon, about sunset, and as the coast now trends much more to the westward, with concave lines from Hatteras to Cape Lookout (near Beaufort), and from Lookout to Cape Fear, our course took us farther out to sea. I woke on Tuesday morning to find the ship pitching heavily and heavy rain sounding loud on the deck over my head, driven by gusts of wind. Doubts as to the reliability of my "sea legs" made me prudently keep my berth till about ten o'clock, when I went on deck to find a dense fog and a high running sea. The rain had ceased, but the succeeding fog was a worse obstacle to navigation. We were nearly at our destination, and were feeling our way slowly along. My "doubts" vanished in the fresh air, and the bit of real seafaring was exhilarating. Most of the cabin passengers, however, failed to show themselves on deck, and the soldiers and officers whom duty kept there did not all enjoy it greatly. The recruiting regulations, just then, allowed transfers to the gunboat service of soldiers who had any experience even in inland navigation, and the impulse to change had made the subject a "burning question," even while we were in the West The inveterate practical jokers now had their opportunity, and a man leaning uneasily over the lee rail was sure to be offered the chance to enlist in the navy, with glowing eulogies of its superior comfort compared with marching in the mud. In the middle of the afternoon we dropped anchor in nine fathoms, but toward evening the fog lifted, and we ran further in, anchoring in seven fathoms, about a mile off the shore.[22] Fort Fisher was abreast of us, on Federal Point, its big parapet looking like a long, low hill, with knobs upon it, rising from the beach of glittering white sand against a background of the pine forest. Admiral Porter's fleet lay at their moorings all around us, a few of the lighter vessels having crossed the bar and run into the mouth of Cape Fear River behind the fort, where the river channel was nearly parallel to the sea beach and less than a mile from it. We were at New Inlet, between Federal Point and Smith

Federal troops landing on the beaches off Fort Fisher.

Island, or rather the long, narrow key which runs northward from the island.
Cape Fear is the sharp southern point of Smith Island, some seven miles south of
where we lay, and the old entrance was south and west of the cape, between the
island and the mainland.[23]

 The landing of the troops was a difficult task, for the roughness of the
sea made it impossible for another vessel to lie alongside the transports, and we
had to resort to the slow and somewhat dangerous method of transferring the

General Alfred H. Terry

men from the ships to a light-draft steamer in the
ship's small boats. A little wharf was on the inner
side of Federal Point, but there the water was so
shallow that even the light-draft propeller could
not get to the wharf, and another transfer had to
be made. Crossing the bar could only be done at
high water or near it, and the time for work was
consequently so much shortened that the whole
of the 8th and 9th was used in landing the
division. At sunset of the 9th the sea went down
enough for the propeller to come alongside; the
headquarters tents and baggage were transferred
to her, and we took leave of the good ship
"Atlantic." By the time this transfer was made,
the tide was too low to let us pass in over the bar,

and we had to pass the night on the dirty propeller, lying outside till eight
o'clock of Friday the 10th, when we ran in at high tide, and after the second
transfer resumed our character of land forces on the sandy shore of North
Carolina. All the saddle horses of the command were, however, upon a freight
ship that did not arrive for several days, and mounted officers who had lived in
the saddle for years found it slow and tiresome work to wade on foot through the
soft sands in the performance of military duty.

General Terry with his forces was holding a line across Federal Point about two miles above Fort Fisher,[25] and I directed my own troops to encamp a little in rear of Terry's line. My own quartermaster arranged with the chief of that department on the ground to send our headquarters tents and baggage with the division. Meanwhile, taking the little river steamboat which had made our final transfer to the shore, I visited General Schofield, who had his headquarters temporarily on the steamer "Spaulding," assigned to the medical department for hospital use, but which at the time had no sick or wounded on board. Like myself, he was for the nonce dismounted, and as he was contemplating movements up both sides of Cape Fear River, some means of ready communication with both banks was a necessity. With him I visited Admiral Porter on the flag-ship "Malvern," and a movement for next day, the 11th, was arranged.[26]

General Bragg was in command of the Confederate Department of North Carolina, to which he was assigned when General Lee, being made by law general-in-chief of the army, superseded him in the similar duties he had been performing by appointment of President Davis. Bragg's

The giant sand dune known as Sugar Loaf, north of Fort Fisher, as it appears a century after Cox saw it. It has been a landmark since the earliest explorers first charted the Cape Fear region of North Carolina.

headquarters were at Wilmington.[27] Hoke's division was mostly in intrenchments across Federal Point about four miles above Fort Fisher, his right resting at Sugar-loaf Hill on the left bank of the river, and his left near the lower end of Myrtle Sound. Opposite Sugar-loaf, at Old Brunswick, was Fort Anderson, a strong earthwork with ten pieces of heavy ordnance, garrisoned by General Hagood with his brigade of two thousand men.[28] The channel of the river was obstructed by torpedoes and other defensive devices. The enemy's fortifications

The U.S.S. Malvern, Admiral David D. Porter's flagship, at Norfolk Naval Yard.

on Smith Island and near Smithville had been abandoned when Fort Fisher fell, opening the way into the river above them.

On board the "Malvern" it was arranged that a monitor and other vessels of the fleet which could cross the bar should ascend the river and engage Fort Anderson, whilst Terry's troops, supported by my division, should make a strong reconnoissance of Hoke's lines and, if they were found to be strongly held, establish counter lines near them, so that most of the forces could then be used for flanking operations.[29] Returning to my command, I found it encamped as had been ordered, and our headquarters tents in comfortable shape by the zealous labors of our servants aided by the headquarters guard. General Terry kindly sent over four horses as a mount for myself and my most necessary staff officers in the movement to begin in the morning. One of the first questions a soldier asks in regard to his camping-place is, Where is water to be got? One's first impression would be that on this flat tongue of sand covered only with a sparse growth of pines and scrub live-oak, with the ocean on one side and a tidal river on the other, fresh water would be scarce and brackish. But we were agreeably disappointed to find that near us, in the middle of the sands, was a juniper swamp and pond of which the water was sweet and wholesome, though from the juniper roots it had the bright brown color of coffee.

On the 11th the movement was made as planned. Hoke's outposts and pickets were driven from their rifle-pits, and his main line at Sugar-loaf well reconnoitred. Terry's new line was established within small-arm range of the enemy and intrenched so that Hoke might be obliged to hold his own position in force. In the advance I was much interested in observing the conduct of the

U.S. Colored Troops, and their commander, Charles Paine (below)

colored troops in General Paine's division, for I had never before seen them in action. They were well disciplined and well led, and went forward with alacrity in capital form, showing that they were good soldiers. I rode well forward purposely to watch their skirmishers, and was greatly pleased to see the pace they took and the lively way in which they followed up the Confederate outposts when once these were started.

When the new position was taken up, I went to the river bank, and there, from a sand breastwork so white that it looked like a snow-drift, I watched with my field-glass a duel between the monitor "Montauk" and Fort Anderson. The monitor, which lay about a mile from the fort, was of the original single-turret form, armed with the large-calibre smooth-bores, which were fired with great deliberation and with surprising accuracy. I could not see how any rifled guns could have improved on their practice. The conical shot would, of course, have

Union ships, including the monitor Montauk, shell Fort Anderson.

Another image of the monitor U.S.S. Montauk.

excelled in penetrating power and in range, but the big round shells seemed to be put just where the gunners wished. A group of men stood on the deck of the monitor behind the turret, and they frequently came out from its cover to watch the effect of the firing, having time to step back again, between the flash of the enemy's gun and the passing of the shot. The deck of the monitor, being almost awash, was no mark at all for the artillerists in the fort, and it would be the merest chance if a ricochet shot struck it. If it did, the very low angle of impact made it fly off without doing any harm. The turret was dented with some centre shots, as I saw when I visited the vessel later, but it was practically impregnable

BGen. Adelbert Ames

to the ordnance the Confederates used. On the other hand, the direct fire from the ship was limited in its effect to the displacement of earth on the parapet or the knocking away of the cheeks of the embrasures. The body of the garrison was kept out of range, and the artillerists were so close to the rampart that when shells exploded over them, the fragments flew beyond and there were few casualties.

General Terry was left to hold the new line established in face of Hoke with Paine's division and Abbott's brigade, whilst my division and Ames's (of Terry's command) were marched back to camp near Fort Fisher. Schofield's own idea had been to send me with my own and Ames's divisions across the river to operate against Fort Anderson by the west bank and, by taking it, force the enemy to evacuate the Sugar-loaf position opposite. By thus concentrating on the bank most weakly held, we would by a sort of see-saw work them back till they must give up Wilmington or fight for it in the open. I was directed to be ready to cross the river on the 12th, but the order was countermanded, and it was determined to try a plan which would avoid the necessity of dividing the forces on the two sides of

Fort Anderson as it appeared from the waters of the Cape Fear River (above), and a map of the Union plan of attack (below). The fort was the last major obstacle to troops advancing on Wilmington in February of 1865.

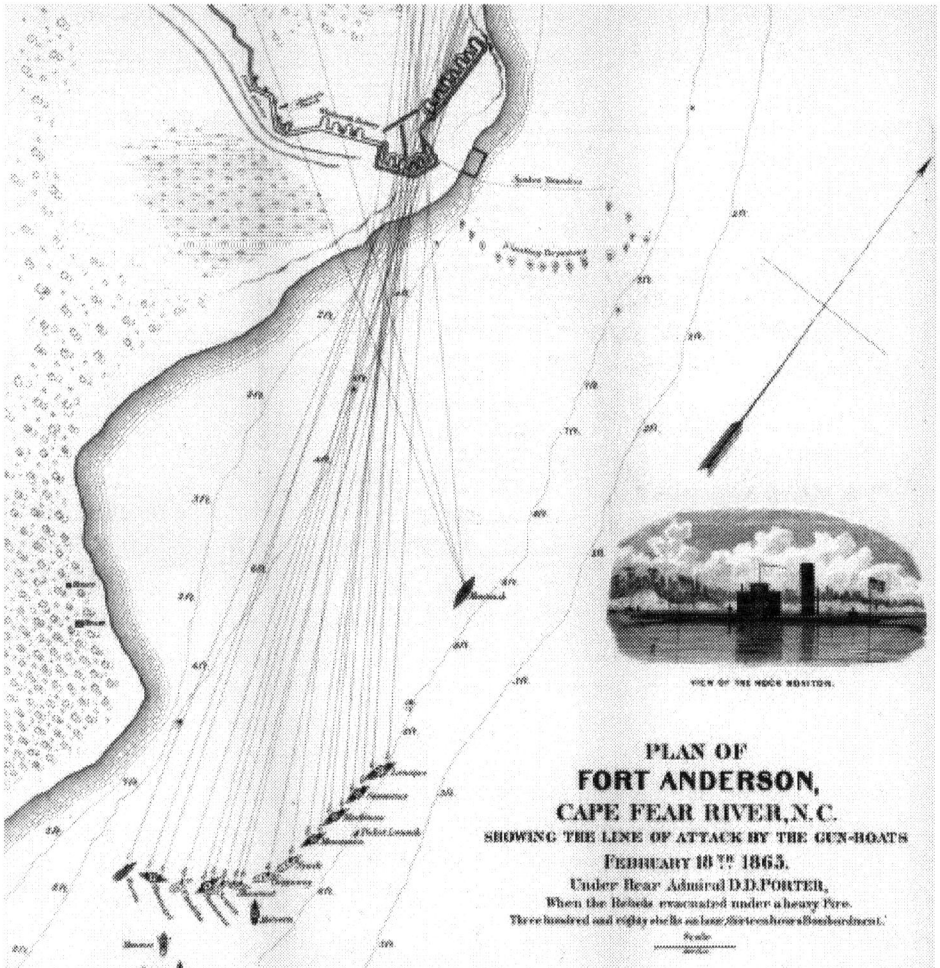

a large river. Colonel Comstock of Grant's staff, who had accompanied Terry as engineer in the taking of Fort Fisher[30] and who was still with us, had made a reconnoissance up the coast on the 11th, and found at Big Hill, three miles south of Masonboro Inlet, a position from which it seemed practicable to cover the collection and launching of enough pontoon boats to ferry a column of troops across Myrtle Sound. If this could be done with secrecy and speed till enough were over to make head against the enemy while the rest were crossing, Hoke's position would be turned and he would have to fall back upon more open country, where our whole force could be manoeuvred against him.

On Comstock's suggestion Schofield determined to try the plan, which was a promising one if winds and waves would permit. The navy was to tow the boats to the place of rendezvous with a body of engineer troops under Comstock's orders, whilst Schofield led Ames's and my divisions by the shore.[31]

Gen. Johnson Hagood, CSA

The movement was made after dark on the evening of the 12th, but the bad weather had hardened down into a regular northeaster, and it proved impossible to tow the pontoon boats through the heavy sea. After a night of severe exposure we returned to camp to find many of our tents flattened by the gale. After a day's rest the effort was renewed on the 14th, but as the admiral reported that the sea was too rough for even the smaller steamers to go outside, the plan was modified so as to try drawing the boats on their trucks, though the number of our draft animals was as yet very small.[32] What with the heavy surf on the beach and the deep, soft sand beyond it, the weak teams could not pull the trucks far, and gave out before we reached the chosen position. As we turned back after midnight the moon was just rising, and the scene was a wild one, with the flying clouds and the foaming waves silvered by the moonlight; but the rarest sight was, just as half the moon's great disk was above the horizon, a ship of war stood against it, exactly framed in the semicircle of light as if drawn in black on the silver surface. The plan was an interesting one and would probably have succeeded in favorable weather, but the winter storm forbade.[33]

Then came the resumption of the original purpose, and I was assigned to command the column advancing from Smithville up the other bank of the river. One brigade of Couch's division (Moore's) had arrived, and it was ordered to report to me. Ames's division was also in the column till Fort Anderson was

Schofield coordinated the advance up the Cape Fear River aboard the hospital ship
Spaulding.

evacuated in the night of the 18th, when it rejoined Terry and I moved on against
the Confederate position at Town Creek.[34] Ferrying the unfordable stream,
Hagood's brigade was attacked and routed on the 20th, capturing two cannon
and nearly 400 prisoners, including Colonel Simonton the commandant, Hagood
himself having gone to Wilmington.[35] On the 21st we pressed on to Brunswick
Ferry, and saved part of the pontoon bridge there which the
enemy had not been able to destroy completely. An
advance-guard was got over on Eagle Island, the large
swampy island lying in front of Wilmington, where
the remnant of Hagood's brigade held the narrow
causeway. Bragg had been to Richmond on an official
visit, but was back at Wilmington and saw that the
time to evacuate had come. The naval stores were set
on fire, and the dense black pillars of smoke from the
warehouses of resin and turpentine told us the story.[36]

My route from Town Creek around
McIlhenny's mill-pond to Brunswick Ferry had taken
me some three miles back from the river, and the
broad swamps and rice-fields intervening made
communication with General Schofield on the
"Spaulding," very slow and difficult.[37] The sequel
well illustrates the importance of complete
confidence on the part of a subordinate that his
chief will sanction and heartily approve the use

MajGen. Robert Hoke, CSA

of full discretion in circumstances where quick and full intercourse is
impossible. By long service with General Schofield, I knew that he was no
martinet, snubbing any independence of action, but an officer of sound and calm

judgment, fairly considering the reasons we might have for any departure from the letter of an order. General Terry's troops were facing the greater part of Hoke's division in a position nearly opposite the mouth of Town Creek, and were meeting with stubborn resistance. It was known that Hardee's command, having evacuated Charleston, was moving northward to unite with the Confederates in North Carolina, and it was supposed to aim at reaching Wilmington. There were rumors that he had already joined Bragg.

In these circumstances General Schofield had said to me, by a dispatch in the morning, "If you can destroy the bridge over Brunswick River or break the railroad to-day, do so, but be ready to cross the river early this evening near the mouth of Town Creek."[38] Early in the afternoon I reported progress, saying: "My head of column reached this place [Brunswick Ferry] about one o'clock. The rebels had partially destroyed their pontoon bridge, but from the creek I got several boats, and have put a regiment over on the island. They got most of the way across, when the enemy opened with one gun, commanding the straight road. As the rest of the island seems impracticably swampy, this checked our reconnoissance; but there can be little doubt the rebels are evacuating. They have made immense fires, the smoke of which you must have seen, indicating that they are destroying turpentine, etc. A few skirmishers were on the opposite side of Brunswick River when we reached it, but they ran at once. The enemy has destroyed all flatboats within reach, but I may hunt some up. I am pushing a reconnoissance further up the river, by way of threatening to cross above the island, and so hasten their movements. I shall put my command in position covering the crossing and the Georgetown road, and watch the movements, in the town. The railroad bridge across Brunswick River is partially destroyed, and we hear the cars on the other side of the town from here. I cannot doubt that General Terry will have an open road in the morning, and think from the general indications that I am entirely secure here. I will face in all directions and get all the intelligence I can, while awaiting orders. There is no railroad or other bridge over Cape Fear River."[39]

Whilst this report was on the road to Schofield, a messenger who left the general about noon was slowly working his way to me, bearing this message: "My last report from General Terry indicates that he will not be able to force the enemy back from the position held by him last evening. General Terry thinks Hoke has his whole force in his front. It will therefore be necessary to transfer your troops to the east bank of the river to-night. The men will be put across in small boats near the mouth of Town Creek, unless Terry succeeds in effecting a lodgment higher up. In the latter event I will signal you. Otherwise move your troops to the mouth of Town Creek without further orders. Let your artillery and animals go down to Fort Anderson. I will have them sent from that place by steamers to Federal Point this evening. If you can destroy the bridges over

Brunswick River to-day, do so; but in any event be ready to commence crossing the river by dusk or earlier, if practicable. You might perhaps send back a brigade or two while the others are doing the work."[40]

At six o'clock, in the dusk of the evening, this letter reached me, and I instantly replied: "Your dispatch directing movement is only just received, the messenger having lost his way. As I am eight miles from the mouth of Town Creek, and it is already dark, your directions cannot be literally followed, and the circumstances impress me so strongly with the belief that the enemy are about to evacuate Wilmington to-night that I venture to send one brigade now and wait further orders before withdrawing all. It will take all night to get the whole command to Town Creek, and it seems impossible to cross them all, beginning at an hour so much later than you anticipated when sending the dispatch. Some engineers on the railroad who have come into my lines, several other citizens, and a number of slaves, all agree in reporting the intention of evacuating immediately. The destruction of immense quantities of property since I came up this evening looks the same way. I have collected and repaired nearly all of the pontoons and materials of the bridge, and had begun relaying them when your dispatch came. I cannot retire my own force now without it appearing a retreat. I would be entirely willing to stay here with one brigade, and should feel quite confident that I could at any time bring it off safely, if we remained here several days even. Thinking you would not desire more troops at Town Creek than you can cross to-night, I ... think it right to send the one brigade, and if more can cross, I can still send them, so as to be not much behind the others if the messenger makes reasonable haste. I believe I mentioned in a former dispatch that the rebels themselves destroyed the Brunswick River railroad bridge."[41]

The orderly who reached me had been landed from a small boat and made his way to me on foot, and as he had eight or nine miles to walk by a wretched road, it was not strange that he was late in reaching me. Giving him his supper whilst I wrote my dispatch, I then mounted him on a horse, and sent with him another mounted man to bring the return message. My first messenger had tried to reach the river through the swamps at several points, but had not succeeded in getting within hailing distance of any vessels in the stream. He happened, however, to fall in with the second messengers in his wanderings, and was now taken to the place where a small boat was to be sent, and so it happened that both my dispatches reached Schofield together, but not till about half-past ten. Meanwhile, the general having heard nothing whatever from me, and getting unfavorable reports from Terry, wrote me again at a quarter-past seven.

He said: "My orderlies and your signal officer seem to have got lost, and I have heard nothing from you since 10.30 A. M. I sent an order to you by an orderly on foot about noon, but do not feel at all certain that it has reached you. I want you to move back abreast of the fleet, just above the mouth of Town Creek, to-night, and be ready to cross the river at dawn of day in the morning. Send all your wagons and horses to Fort Anderson. The men will cross in small boats. Better send a regiment with your wagons, horses, and artillery. Should the enemy be in force in your front, it might be necessary to cross Town Creek before crossing the river. About this, act according to your judgment. I intended you to cross the river to-night, but it is now too late."[42]

But whilst this last orderly was on his dark and weary way to me, my two dispatches finally got through, and at 10.20 Schofield wrote me from the cabin of the "Spaulding" as follows: "Your dispatch of 6 P.M. is just received, and is highly satisfactory. The one of an earlier date, but the hour not given, came at the same time. About seven o'clock I sent another to you directing you to come back. I hope this will reach you in time to take its place. My orders were based on General Terry's report of an increase of the force in his front, and that of prisoners that Hardee's forces had arrived from Charleston. I think you would certainly have learned it if the latter were true That you have sent one brigade back is well. You may send another as soon as you get this dispatch. Keep the other two where you are until daylight in the morning. Then, if the rebels have gone, you can enter the town, taking care to hold the river crossings. If the enemy has not gone, or you are not positive that he is going, then move back and cross the river as before directed."[43]

Immediately after this, Schofield wrote me another dispatch, briefer, but of the same general purport.[44] It was probably sent by way of precaution, in case any accident happened to the bearer of the other. Arrangements had been made to get over some horsemen so as to speed these dispatches, and they came through to me by midnight. But meanwhile my perplexity as to my duty was intensified. I had put over the Sixteenth Kentucky upon Eagle Island, and made them throw up a breastwork across the cause-way facing that of the enemy, which was near the main channel of Cape Fear River. They were exploring the swamps, seeking information and preparing to force the position in the morning. My confidence in my forecast was such that I did not cease work on the repair of the pontoons, and had the crossing ready for use late in the evening, but awaited further orders with great anxiety. At 11.45, however, came the order dated at 7.15, reiterating the direction to withdraw. Moore's brigade had gone under the first order, Henderson's was waiting ready to march, and I started it for Town Creek.[45] Reilly's (Colonel Sterl in command) began to follow. The march in a dark night made it proper to leave reasonable intervals between the brigades, and I was still waiting with Casement's brigade, and had not destroyed the pontoon bridge, when, at midnight, I got Schofield's dispatch of 10.20, which had come through in less than half the time other messages had taken, under his eager orders to force the horses through at speed. I at once recalled Sterl, and with great satisfaction wrote to the General, "Your dispatch of 10.20 received in time to stop two brigades. Henderson's and Moore's have gone forward and will report at the river above Town Creek. I will inform you of any changes in the morning. The railroad employes who came in to me informed me positively that Hardee's troops had not come here."[46] My outpost on the island was replaced, and before day dawned we knew that the last of the enemy had disappeared from our immediate front and that Wilmington was evacuated. Bragg had carefully removed all boats from our side of the channel, but citizens anxious to prevent us from firing on the town came over in skiffs, and we learned that the Confederate forces had marched away toward Goldsborough, leaving the way open for Terry's march into the city, which took place in the early morning of the 22d, which we were happy to recall was Washington's Birthday.

It has seemed worth while to give the correspondence at such length, because it well illustrates the difficulties under which officers must labor in war, and the necessity for a good deal of freedom of action and of discretion in deciding upon his course, when the commander of a detached column finds his communication with headquarters obstructed and retarded by accidental circumstances. Had General Schofield's methods been rigid in requiring literal obedience, my command would have abandoned the advantages we had gained, and the campaign might have taken quite another turn. My complete confidence in the liberality of his judgment when the facts should be all known, encouraged me to a course which would otherwise have been impossible.[47] There was with me a very efficient squad of the Signal Corps, under Lieutenant Ketchum, which had kept up flag communication with the "Spaulding" and across the river in our advance from Smithville to Town Creek, but when we advanced to Brunswick Ferry, Mr. Ketchum found it impossible, on account of the course of Brunswick River and the dense woods upon the banks, to establish any station from which he could communicate with any of the vessels in the river below, or with General Terry on the east bank of the Cape Fear.[48] This threw us unexpectedly upon messengers as the only go-betweens, and led to the embarrassments which have been described.

Chapter XLVI Notes:

1. Official Records, vol. xlvii. pt. ii. p. 131.
2. *Id.*, vol. xlv. pt. ii. pp. 529, 586.
3. To get an adequate idea of the task of transporting an army corps so great a distance, one should look at Colonel Parsons's report, including 250 dispatches. Official Records, vol. xlvii. pt. ii. pp. 215-284.
4. *Id.*, vol. xlv. pt. ii. p. 596.

5. *Id.*, vol. xlvii. pt. ii. p. 102.

6. Official Records, vol. xlvii. pt. ii. pp. 121, 179, 190, 201.

7. See Sherman Letters, p. 245.

8. Official Records, vol. xlvii. pt. ii. p. 103. In the same letter Sherman referred to the farewell order General Butler had addressed to his troops on being relieved of command. "I am rejoiced that Terry took Fisher," Sherman said, "because it silences Butler, who was to you a dangerous man. His address to his troops on being relieved was a direct, mean, and malicious attack on you, and I admired the patience and skill by which you relieved yourself and the country of him." In the address referred to, Butler had said: "I have been chary of the precious charge confided to me. I have refused to order the useless sacrifice of the lives of such soldiers, and I am relieved from your command. The wasted blood of my men does not stain my garments." (O. R, vol. xlvi. pt. ii. p. 71.) Such a publication made its author liable to court-martial, but Grant took no public notice of it, except to oppose his further assignment to duty. *Id.*, vol. xlvii. pt. ii. pp. 537, 562. See also Sherman to Admiral Porter, *Id.*, p. 104, and Grant to Sherman, *Id.*, p. 859.

9. *Id.*, p. 193.

10. *Id.*, vol. xliv. p. 809, and Sherman's Memoirs, vol. ii. p. 166.

11. Official Records, vol. xlvii. pt. ii. p. 18.

12. *Id.*, p. 155.

13. For connected historical treatment of Sherman's march northward, and of the capture of Fort Fisher, see "March to the Sea," etc., chaps, viii.-xi.: Life of Sherman (Great Commanders' Series), chap. xii.

14. Official Records, vol. xlvii. pt. ii. p. 154.

15. Official Records, vol. xlvii. pt. ii. p. 194.

16. Official Records, vol. xlvii. pt. ii. p. 135.

17. *Id.*, pp. 116, 119, 126, 204, 293.

18. *Id.*, p. 213.

19. *Id.*, p. 293.

20. *Id.*, p. 284.

21. As the Records do not seem to contain many orders for the conduct of troops on transport ships, I insert that which I made for this voyage. It was, of course, supplemental to the Army Regulations of 1863, chap, xxxvii.

"Special Orders No. 9.

HEADQUARTERS, THIRD DIV., 23D ARMY CORPS,(Steamship Atlantic, February 4, 1865.

The following regulations will be strictly observed by the officers and men of this command during the present voyage:

1. No open lights will be allowed in any part of the ship occupied by troops. The ship's lanterns will be arranged by the officers of the vessel in such a way as to light the decks during the night, and will not be opened or interfered with by the men.

2. No smoking will be allowed in any part of the vessel used for sleeping except the open decks. The men may smoke in the open air upon the upper decks, and the brigade commander will provide for giving proper airing, and opportunity to smoke, to the men quartered below. Officers will smoke, either upon deck or in the smoking-room near the water-closets.

3. The division and brigade commissaries will make arrangements with the steward of the ship for cooking the men's coffee and doing other necessary cooking for the command, and for serving the same out at regular hours.

4. The canteens of the men may be filled with drinking water once each day, the men being marched by companies under their proper officers to the pump in the fore part of the ship for that purpose.

5. The brigade commander, in consultation with the commander of the ship, will arrange for the perfect policing of the quarters, sinks, etc.

6. The starboard side of the upper and main decks abaft of the engine, will be kept clear of men and reserved for the use of officers, both of the command and of the ship, during the day; and such portion of this space as may necessarily be occupied by the men for sleeping at night, will have a passage kept entirely clear for the use of the officers and crew of the vessel in working her at night. No men will at any time be allowed to go upon the roofs of the houses on the upper deck.

7. Proper roll-calls will be established, and the line officers will be strictly required to attend them, and to make close personal inspections daily of the condition of their men, and to be personally in command of them when marched out for water, or coffee, or when on duty.

8. An officer of the day will be daily appointed by the brigade commander, and shall have full charge of the execution of this order, and supervision of all the police arrangements of the command. Proper line officers will be detailed on guard duty, and sentries will be regularly posted at the bulkhead of the ship storeroom on the forward lower deck, at the sinks, over the lights at night, and on the middle line of the decks reserved under paragraph six.

9. The officer of the day, after reporting at brigade headquarters each day, will report to the captain of the ship, in order that the ship's officers may know to whom to apply for any enforcement of these regulations.

By command of Major-General Cox.

(Signed) THEO. Cox,(Capt. and Ass't Adj't-General."

Official Records, vol. xlvii. pt. ii. p. 303.

22. Official Records, vol. xlvii. pt. i. p. 927.
23. See official Atlas, pl. cxxxix.
24. Official Records, vol. xlvii. pt. i. p. 910.
26. Official Records, vol. xlvii. pt. i. p. 927.
27. Official Records, vol. xlvii. pt. ii. pp. 1088, 1099.
28. Official Atlas, pl. cxxxii.; Official Records, vol. xlvii. pt. i. pp. 911, 1077.
29. *Id.*, p. 958.
30. Official Records, vol. xlvi. pt. ii. p. 30.
31. Official Records, vol. xlvii. pt. ii. pp. 403,404.
32. *Id.*, pp. 426, 427.
33. Official Records, vol. xlvii. pt. ii. p. 437.
34. *Id.*, pt. i. p. 960; pt. ii. pp. 492, 493.
35. *Id.*, pp. 495, 509.
36. *Id.*, pp. 1241-1245.
37. Official Atlas, pl. cxxxii.
38. Official Records, vol. xlvii. pt. ii. p. 520
39. Official Records, vol. xlvii. pt. ii. p. 521.
40. *Ibid.*
41. Official Records, vol. xlvii. pt. ii. p. 522.
42. Official Records, vol. xlvii. pt. ii. p. 522.
43. Official Records, vol. xlvit. pt. ii. p. 522.
44. *Id.*, p. 523.
45. *Id.*, p. 524.
46. Official Records, vol. xlvii. pt. ii. p. 523.
47. In 1870 Moltke had adopted the wise rule of leaving to subordinates of the higher grades very large discretion, and to avoid trammelling them by detailed orders or by prematurely communicated plans. "The very lack of instructions gave them liberty and imposed on them the duty of acting on their own responsibility, in case unforeseen events should require such prompt action that orders from the Supreme Commander could not be waited for." (Hohenlohe-Ingelfingen, Strategy, vol. i. p. 324.) It was even looked upon as "an unwarranted censure" on the subordinate "if anything was enjoined unnecessarily," or which was within the proper knowledge and discretion of the officer. *Id.*, vol. ii. p. 39.
48. Official Records, vol. xlvii. pt. i. pp. 915, 916.

CHAPTER XLVII

THE CONFEDERACY IN STRAITS—JOHNSTON COMMANDS IN THE
CAROLINAS—OUR OPERATIONS FROM NEW BERNE—BATTLE OF
KINSTON

The Confederates lose Charleston and Columbia—Facing a crisis—Hopeless
apathy of Southern people—Mr. Davis's perplexity—Beauregard startles him—
Lee calls Johnston to command—Personal relations of leading officers—
Dwindling armies—The cavalry—Assignments of generals—The Beaufort and
New Berne line—Am ordered to New Berne—Provisional corps—Advance to
cover railway building—Dover and Gum swamps—Bragg concentrates to
oppose us—Position near Kinston—Bragg's plan of attack—Our own
movements—Condition of railroad and river—Our advance to Wise's Forks and
Southwest Creek—Precautions—Conference with Schofield—Battle of
Kinston—Enemy attack our left front—Rout of Upham's brigade—Main line
firm—Ruger's division reaches the field—Enemy repulsed—End of first day's
fight—Extending our trenches on the left—Sharp skirmishing of the 9th—
Bragg's reinforcements—His attack of the both—Final repulse and retreat of the
enemy.

Upon our occupation of Wilmington, Bragg retreated northward along the
line of the railroad toward Goldsborough, which was the crossing of the
Wilmington and Weldon Railway with that from New Berne to Raleigh.
Sherman had captured the capital of South Carolina, and in his movement
northward his left wing had followed the railroad from Columbia toward
Charlotte, N. C, as far as Winnsborough, forty miles, for the purpose of making a

permanent break in that line of communication before turning his columns eastward toward Cheraw and Fayetteville on his way to Goldsborough, the rendezvous he had fixed for his junction with Schofield's army. Beauregard, whose command now included South Carolina,[1] had moved with the forces under his immediate command from Augusta, through Columbia to Charlotte, and was calling to him all the Confederate troops operating against Sherman.[2] On the 14th of February he had ordered Hardee to evacuate Charleston, and the unwelcome proof that South Carolina was lost so alarmed Mr. Davis that he urged Hardee to hold on as long as possible. But both Lee and Beauregard became uneasy lest Hardee should be caught before he could join the rest, and despite Mr. Davis's bitter disappointment, the evacuation was made in the night of the 17th, Hardee being sick abed for a few days, and turning over the command to General McLaws.[3]

Generals Braxton Bragg (above) and P.G.T. Beauregard (below)

The loss of Charleston, the original cradle of secession, seemed a portent to the people of the South, and well-nigh destroyed all hope. Governor Magrath of South Carolina had written Mr. Davis, a month before, that the fate of the Confederacy was involved in the early movements of Sherman's march from Savannah, and that he was in earnest correspondence with the Governors of North Carolina and Georgia, urging extraordinary efforts. "Richmond will surely fall when Charleston is lost," he said, adding emphatically, "To retain Richmond until Charleston is lost is to sacrifice both."[4] Davis was not blind to the consequences, or to the nature of the crisis. A week before Magrath's letter was written, the Confederate President had sent a dispatch to Governor Brown of Georgia, declaring the absolute necessity of making Hardee strong enough to stop Sherman on the line of the Combahee, which he rightly said was stronger than any position that could be occupied further north. He ended with the appeal, "We must look forward, and leave discussions of the past to a more convenient season."[5] Governor Vance of North Carolina issued a proclamation powerfully appealing to his people for a final rally, using the failure of the recent peace conference at Fort Monroe as proof that there was only subjugation offered us, the mere details of which they [Lincoln and Seward] proposed to settle.[6] But the whole South was already in apathetic despair under the conviction of their helplessness to check the triumphant march of Sherman's 60,000 veterans or prevent his junction with Schofield's 30,000. Instead of growing by an enthusiastic rally of the old men and the boys, the Southern army was dwindling by steady small streams of deserters, no longer able to repress the impulse to go to their helpless families within the Union lines.[7] The appeals of the governors produced no result, or only called out responses in the press, never ventured before, saying the desperate efforts had already been made, the physical power of the States was exhausted, it was vain to talk of independence, it was time to make real overtures for peace.[8]

The military outlook for the South was certainly gloomy enough. Distrusting Beauregard's ability to deal with his perplexing problem, Mr. Davis had asked Lee (on the 19th) whether it was possible for him to get away from Petersburg long enough to go to Beauregard and advise him after a personal conference.[9] But Lee could not leave his post for a moment with any confidence that Grant's iron grip would not crush the defences of Petersburg and bring the final struggle. Davis became still more troubled when, on the 21st, Beauregard sent him a dispatch indicating his belief that Lee must join him at Salisbury with part of his forces, say 20,000 men, give Sherman battle there," crush him, then to concentrate all forces against Grant, and then to march on Washington to dictate a peace." Beauregard's evident opinion that he was wholly unable to cope with Sherman was much more depressing than his light-hearted

Jefferson Davis

suggestion of marching on Washington to dictate a peace was inspiring. Davis sent it to Lee, saying it was "of a startling character," and urged that the General-in-Chief should direct the concentration of the forces in the Carolinas. He sent also General Gilmer, his chief of engineers, to Beauregard to examine the situation, to advise with him and report.[10]

In this condition of affairs, Beauregard's retreat into North Carolina, where Bragg commanded and was senior in rank, made a new complication; whilst the fall of Wilmington and the danger of Hardee's being cut off before he could unite with the Confederate forces trying to resist Sherman, made a climax of embarrassments which imperatively required the appointment of some one to command in chief in the Carolinas. The same current of opinion in the Confederate Congress which had resulted in Lee's assignment by law (February 9th)[11] to command all the Confederate armies, indicated General Johnston for the post second in importance. Indeed, the knowledge of Mr. Davis's determination not to intrust Johnston with another army in the field entered into the motives for taking the military command out of the President's hands, for it was understood that Lee believed Johnston to be the man best fitted for the second place. Action could be no longer delayed, and the very day of our occupation of Wilmington, Lee telegraphed to Johnston to assume command, concentrate all available forces, and drive back Sherman.[12] For the moment Bragg was not directed to report to Johnston, but consideration for the unpleasant personal relations between them since the Atlanta campaign could not stand long in the way. Beauregard accepted loyally his subordination to Johnston, and, his health not being very strong, was assigned at his own request to administrative duties at Raleigh, including the collection and forwarding of troops, their supply in the field and the management of the relations to the civil authorities of North Carolina, with nominal position of second in command.[13]

Gen. Joseph Johnston, CSA (above) and Gen. William T. Sherman, USA (below).

Johnston had been at Lincolnton, N. C., when notified of his appointment, and in accepting the call to duty, gave his opinion that it was too late to concentrate troops enough to drive back Sherman. He promised, however, to learn from Beauregard the actual situation, and to do all in his power to collect the army and resist Sherman's advance.[14] He met Beauregard at Charlotte, and on the 25th of February assumed command. As to his means of resistance, the returns show a significant dwindling in each of his corps. Hardee had reported, on January 20th, 25,290 present for duty in his department.[15] Hood's army at Tupelo, at the same date, returned 18,708 infantry and artillery, which were soon nearly all in motion for the Carolinas.[16] Bragg's return for his command in North Carolina on February 10th was 11,206.[17] Besides these, there were some militia from Georgia and South Carolina estimated at 1450,[18] and Butler's division of cavalry, more than 3000 strong, had been sent from Lee's army in Virginia.[19] Here were, then, between 55,000 and 60,000 men apparently available to oppose Sherman, and making a larger army than the Confederate generals attributed to him when he started from Savannah.[20] It was not strange, therefore, that when, at a conference of Beauregard with Hardee and others in Augusta on February 3d, the troops relied on for the campaign were estimated at 33,450,[21] Mr. Davis noted by his indorsement on the paper that the previous returns showed a larger force present for duty.[22] He however added that the language "relied on as effectives" might account for the difference. But when on the 21st Beauregard, in the dispatch proposing that Lee should send part of his army to Salisbury, N. C., said, "Hardee and myself can collect about 15,000 exclusive of Cheatham and Stewart, not likely to reach in time,"[23] the startling effect on the Confederate

Gen. Wade Hampton, CSA

President was the most natural thing in the world. Armies seemed to vanish in thin air.

On taking command, Johnston had accepted his predecessor's estimates of both his own forces and those of Sherman. From Charlotte, N. C., he wrote Lee that his opponent now seemed to be moving eastward, aiming at Fayetteville. This place he thought he might make the point of concentration for Hardee's troops, coming from Charleston to Cheraw by railroad, and those with Beauregard, which were in the main the divisions of Hood's army, coming forward piecemeal, and now amounting to something over 9000 men. He suggested that Bragg should join him at Fayetteville also.[24] The Confederate cavalry was now led by Wade Hampton, who was made lieutenant-general to

outrank Wheeler, who was not regarded equal to the responsibility. The latter
retained two divisions, and the rank of corps commander under Hampton.[25] As
soon as it was evident that Sherman was likely to reach the North Carolina
border, Johnston was authorized to control Bragg's operations also.[26] This was,
of course, a personal grief to the latter, who asked to be relieved; but in the
critical condition of affairs personal feelings had to give way, and Bragg's
request went unanswered.[27] He did not insist upon it and gave loyal support to
Johnston. General D. H. Hill had been sent from Virginia to report to
Beauregard, and was commanding at Augusta, Ga., when Sherman's march
eastward from Columbia relieved Augusta from danger, and Hill at his own
request was ordered to join Beauregard. S. D. Lee was absent from his corps by
reason of a wound he had received at Nashville, and Hill was assigned to its
temporary command.[28] The growing decay of discipline and organization was
shown by the irregularity of reports, and for the few weeks the war still went on,
Johnston had to content himself with abbreviated returns, which contained only
the numbers of effectives and aggregates present.[29] Even these were not
regularly sent up, and could not be made to agree with the lists of paroles when
the surrender finally occurred.[30]

Upon our occupation of Wilmington, Schofield turned his attention at
once to the opening, of the line from Beaufort and New Berne to Kinston and
Goldsborough. Terry's troops were sent to follow Bragg northward. Couch's
division of the Twenty-third Corps joined mine at Wilmington. Meagher's
provisional command of detachments of Sherman's army had reached New
Berne; but its commander had given such dissatisfaction by his failure to remain
with it and conduct its shipment from Annapolis, that Grant directed that he
should be relieved and sent home. Such had been the result of a spicy
correspondence between Grant and Halleck which called up poor Meagher's
notorious failings.[31] Schofield had asked for the assignment of Terry to a corps to
comprise the troops in the department not belonging to the Twenty-third Corps,
and of myself to the permanent command of the latter corps;[32] but, pending
action on this, he determined to send me to New Berne to take command of the
so-called District of Beaufort and the troops assembling there, which would
constitute three divisions.[33] General Palmer, who had been there for a long time,
coming in the small steamer "Escort" to visit Schofield and consult concerning
the advance from that base, I went back with him, and was accompanied by
General Carter, whose coming from Tennessee has already been mentioned and
who was to supersede Meagher.[34] As my assignment to this duty was intended to
be temporary, I took only part of my staff with me, and assigned General Reilly,
who had now joined us, to the temporary command of the division. General
Couch was assigned to command the two divisions of our corps which were at
Wilmington.[35] A storm delayed the departure of the "Escort" from Cape Fear

Inlet, but we reached New Berne in the evening of the last day of February. Next day I formally assumed command and organized the forces, distributing the garrison troops and Meagher's men between the two divisions to be commanded by Palmer and Carter, but keeping Ruger's division of the Twenty-third Corps intact. This last had been sent direct to Beaufort and arrived there about the same time with myself. It had not been with us on the Cape Fear River. An immediate advance was ordered for the 2d of March, to cover the work of railroad building.[37]

Colonel Wright, chief of railway construction, had joined Sherman at Savannah, and from thence had been sent to Schofield to rebuild the New Berne-Goldsborough road under his directions.[38] Palmer's forces occupied a position at Batchelder's Creek, nine miles above New Berne on the road to Kinston, and the railroad building began there. Had we been well provided with wagon-trains, it would have been easy to march at once to Kinston, on the left bank of the Neuse, a little over thirty miles from Newberne, and hold that place whilst the railroad was built, obstructions removed from the river, and easy communications opened both by rail and by water. But we were almost destitute of wagons, having only ten to a division. This tied us close to the end of the rails, for after carrying our necessary baggage to the camping-place, it was the utmost the few wagons could do to bring rations and ammunition a very few miles from the nearest temporary station on the railroad. Dover and Gum swamps were practically continuous to within three

Gen. Daniel Harvey Hill, CSA

miles of Kinston, and steady rains had put most of the road under water.[39] This necessarily slow progress gave the enemy time to arrange for concentrating upon us.

The importance of trying to check our columns advancing from the sea-coast was seen by General Johnston as soon as he learned the situation in North Carolina. On the 3d of March, when he supposed Schofield to be continuing his movements up Cape Fear River, he had inquired of Bragg whether it were not feasible to interpose between Schofield and Hardee.[40] As soon as it was known that Schofield was not marching against Hardee, Bragg sent Hoke with his

Military trains played a key role in the strategies of both sides in North Carolina.

division to Kinston, and on the 6th telegraphed to Johnston that my forces were advancing and were within nine miles of the town. He believed that the union with him of the troops near Goldsborough would "insure a victory."[41] Johnston immediately ordered all the forces he was moving towards Hardee to report to Bragg at Goldsborough for use in a quick effort to defeat us, with the purpose of uniting them with Hardee immediately afterward to strike at Sherman's advancing columns.[42] It was boldly conceived, and was manifestly the best plan the circumstances admitted. All the detachments of the Army of Tennessee were hurried without change of cars toward Kinston. D. H. Hill had command of them as ranking officer present. It was not pleasant for him to report to Bragg, for a bitter quarrel begun in the Chickamauga campaign had never been appeased, and in giving him the order, Johnston added, "I beg you to forget the past for this emergency."[43] From Davis downward, personal griefs had to be smothered in the crisis, and it is due to them all to remember that they did work together earnestly for their dying cause.

On the 7th of March, Hill reached Kinston with Lee's corps. Hoke's division had preceded him and advanced to Southwest Creek and occupied the lines of intrenchments earlier made along its left bank. This stream was a tributary of the Neuse River and was then unfordable. It described roughly a curve with a radius of about three miles around Kinston, and had for a long time been regarded as the principal defensive line against National troops advancing from New Berne. Several roads radiated from Kinston, crossing Southwest Creek. The Neuse road kept near the bank of the river, going east. Then came the railroad following a nearly straight line to New Berne. The Dover road forked from the Neuse road not far from the town, and took a devious way through the swamps in the same general direction. The upper Trent road ran more nearly south toward Trenton, and followed the course of the Trent River. The Wilmington road went southwesterly toward the city of that name. The several bridges over the creek were from a mile to two miles apart, but had been destroyed or dismantled, and earthworks for artillery had been prepared commanding them. The whole constituted a formidable line of fieldworks when held by an adequate force. Whitford's brigade and a detachment of cavalry had been the only Confederate force at Kinston at the beginning of our campaign, but Bragg had now assembled there Hagood's brigade, which had numbered 2000 in front of Wilmington, and a similar force of North Carolina militia under General Baker, besides Hill and Hoke.[44] Johnston had also informed Bragg that Cheatham's corps and more than half of Stewart's were on the way by rail, under the same orders as Hill's.[45] These constituted in fact all of Johnston's army except Hardee's column, which was still in South Carolina.

The necessity for haste was such, however, that upon Hill's arrival in the night of the 7th, Bragg determined to attack me at once, in the belief that he was strong enough to do so successfully. Hill's corps was accordingly marched to Southwest Creek before day, and relieved Hoke's division in the works extending from the Dover road crossing to the railroad, whilst Hoke, with Clayton's division of Lee's corps besides his own, marched to the upper Trent and Wilmington bridges with orders to sweep down and attack my lines in flank and rear. The plank had been relaid on the bridges which had been held by outposts, and a new bridge had been built of felled trees between the Dover road bridge and the railroad. At the sound of Hoke's attack, Hill was to cross by the last-mentioned bridges, and fall upon our front with all the rest of the Confederate forces.[46]

On our side, Colonel Wright had found that some miles of the railroad had only been partially destroyed, and as iron for six miles had been received when I reached New Berne, he was able to put seven miles of track in passable condition by the evening of the 4th.[47] On that day I had concentrated at Core Creek, twenty miles from New Berne by the wagon roads, and the head of the rails was only one or two miles behind. On the 6th Palmer's and Carter's divisions were advanced to Gum Swamp, seven miles further, taking four days' rations, and Ruger's was to follow on the 7th. On this march I found that for five miles beyond Core Creek the railway had only been capsized, ties and rails together, and was lying in the ditch by the roadside.[48] Relying on the more rapid construction this would enable Colonel Wright to make, I ordered a still further advance for the 7th, hoping to reach Southwest Creek. There we must expect to halt for several days, for the total destruction of the railroad for the last ten or twelve miles from Kinston made it probable that a mile a day was the utmost the construction corps could rebuild, to say nothing of the bridging which would also be necessary.

The Confederate ironclad C.S.S. Neuse was built and berthed at Kinston.

For our own sake, as well as to provide for getting forward large quantities of supplies for Sherman's army when we should join him, it would be necessary to organize a line of river transportation to supplement the railroad. Heavy obstructions to navigation had been placed in the Neuse River, a little above New Berne, as a defence against an iron-clad ram the Confederates had built at Kinston. As, however, she could only come down the river on a freshet, owing to her great draft, I had, upon leaving New Berne, ordered that the obstructions be removed, and light-draft steamboats and flats procured to bring supplies to some point near our camp, or to ferry troops across if I found it advisable to shift my line of operations to the north bank of the river.[49]

On Tuesday, the 7th, the command was in motion, Palmer's division following the railroad, except Claassen's brigade, which had been sent the previous afternoon by the Dover road to Wise's Forks, where it crosses the lower Trent road, which ran diagonally across our front toward the Neuse River. In the skirmish at Wise's Forks, and from a deserter, it was learned that Hoke had joined the Kinston forces with his division, and there were rumors of other reinforcements arriving. Advancing along the railroad, Palmer reached the drier ground near Southwest Creek and came under artillery fire from guns intrenched on the other side of the creek. The country here was wooded, and was traversed by an old road, called the British road, running parallel to the creek from half a mile to a mile from it. The lower Trent road also crossed the railroad not far from the British road crossing. Palmer halted his line in front of the British road covering all the crossings, and advanced outposts and pickets to the creek. Boughton's brigade was on the left of the railroad, and Harland's on the right. The latter detached a regiment to the Neuse road to guard against any attempt by the enemy to cross the creek beyond our right. Major Dow of my staff was also sent with a troop of cavalry to reconnoitre the banks of the river, seeking for a place where steamboats might land supplies and communicate with us.[50] Ruger's division moved forward from Core Creek to Gum Swamp.

On my left, the Twelfth New York Cavalry, Colonel Savage, reconnoitred both Trent roads, under orders to reach out as far to the south as they could, covering Claassen's position at Wise's Forks and giving early notice of any hostile movement in the vicinity. Carter's division delayed its march till it could load up with rations and then followed the Dover road to Claassen's position. On reaching Wise's Forks we found that Claassen had most of his brigade at the crossing of the British road in front, with a detachment of 300 men at Jackson's Mills, where the Dover road crossed the creek. He had smaller detachments also upon the British road on both flanks.[51] I directed General Carter to relieve Claassen's brigade with one of his, that Claassen might rejoin Palmer and make the latter strong enough to spare a detachment to test the condition of the Neuse road crossing of the creek and the presence of the enemy there. Carter sent Upham's brigade to the British road crossing to relieve Claassen, and put the other two in line across the Dover road in front of Wise's Forks, Malloy's on the right of the road and Splaine's on the left with a recurved flank. Upham seems to have marched the whole of his brigade to Jackson's Mills and to have left only a picket post at the British road. He established a skirmish line in rifle-pits close to the creek, and placed a section of artillery which was with him where it would command the bridge site on the Dover road. His picket line connected with Palmer's division on the right, and with the outpost at the British road on the left.[52] Toward evening the cavalry reported that they had found a picket post of the enemy at the bridge on the upper Trent road, had driven it off, taken up the plank of the bridge and piled them on the hither side of the creek, and had established there a picket of their own. Their scouting parties reported no enemy at the Wilmington road crossing.[53] The division commanders were directed to have Southwest Creek in front carefully reconnoitred, to find narrow places where an infantry crossing might be made by an improvised bridge of felled trees.[54]

My habit was to keep my own headquarters well at the front, and I had purposed moving them from Gum Swamp to Wise's Forks on the 7th, but during the day I received word that General Schofield had arrived at Beaufort from Wilmington, coming by sea. We arranged that he should come up for a consultation with me next morning, and to facilitate this, I left my headquarters with Ruger's division, and after a personal visit to Palmer and Carter, I rode back to Gum Swamp in the evening. General Schofield was to come up to the end of the track on the railroad in the morning, and I sent led horses to meet him.[55] The telegraph was made to keep pace with the progress of the railway, and from its upper station we had the aid of flag signals along the railroad bed to Palmer's headquarters.[56] The information we had received of Hoke's presence made it all the more important that we should get out of the swamps, where we could only operate by head of column, to the drier region along Southwest Creek, where the lower Trent road and the British road would give us communication between our flanks and some chance to manoeuvre. These reasons had made me push forward on the 7th, though the movement put us ten miles above the head of the rails and made it sure that we should be short of supplies. As soon as the troops were in position the few wagons with them were unloaded and hurried back, first for ammunition and then for rations.[57] We then had no knowledge of the arrival of any part of Hood's army in North Carolina, and although my provisional corps was far short of being solidly organized, and the troops were either new or unused to field service, I felt no concern lest Hoke should take the offensive alone.

General Schofield had joined me at Gum Swamp about nine o'clock on the morning of the 8th, and after our conference we had mounted to ride to General Palmer's headquarters to see what prospect there might be for securing a crossing near the railroad which would permit preparation for rebuilding the railroad bridge. A note now came from General Carter at Wise's Forks telling of information received from a negro that a large body of the enemy had crossed Southwest Creek at the Wilmington road early in the morning. As the cavalry had a picket at the upper Trent bridge and were supposed to be patrolling beyond the Wilmington road, the information did not seem threatening, but I sent back directions to have the cavalry ordered to do their work thoroughly by instantly testing the truth of the information. Carter was also ordered to support the cavalry with a regiment of infantry.[58] The message from the front was followed almost instantly by another, saying that a heavy force of the enemy had penetrated between Upham's brigade and the rest of the division, almost simultaneously with a report from the cavalry that their picket had been driven from the bridge at the Trent road. As that picket was two miles in front of Upham's left on the British road, it was too evident that the duty of the horsemen had not been well done. Ruger was ordered to march his division at speed to the front, and we galloped to Wise's Forks.[59]

The account I have before given of the enemy's dispositions for the day's work[60] makes it easy to understand the situation as we found it. Hoke, with his own and Clayton's divisions, had turned northward on the British road after getting over Southwest Creek, and as he approached the Dover road, had deployed and advanced upon Upham's flank. The latter, upon the first intimation of an enemy's approach, had hurried the Twenty-seventh Massachusetts to the British road and placed it in line about a quarter of a mile south of the Dover road, which was, of course, his connection with the rest of the division. He also ordered to the same point the section of artillery, and directed the left battalion of his other regiment (Fifteenth Connecticut) to change front also to the south. These orders were judicious, but the odds were too great to make them successful. Far outflanked on either hand, the Massachusetts regiment was put to rout, all the horses of one of the guns were killed, and though the men cut the

The Battle of Kinston.

traces and tried to save the gun by hand, they had to abandon it, while the other retreated on the run toward the main position.[61] General Hill had crossed the creek at the improvised bridge on hearing the sound of Hoke's engagement, but finding a swamp between him and Upham's right, had to make a circuit of it, driving back our pickets in the interval between Carter's and Palmer's divisions. Turning toward the noise of Hoke's firing, he intercepted the right battalion of Upham's Connecticut regiment, and took many of them prisoners.[62] Most of the rest of the regiment finding Hoke's division partly surrounding them, and all other retreat cut off by Hill, surrendered to Hoke. Colonel Upham and most of the Massachusetts regiment succeeded in reaching our main lines, though in confusion. All this was not done, however, without fighting, which took time, and as the whole engagement was in forest or swamp, the enemy was a good deal delayed in his movements and in rectification of lines.

When we reached the field Carter had gone in person toward Upham's position, having first sent a regiment forward on the Dover road to try to reopen communication with him. Palmer was ordered to send his reserve brigade rapidly to extend his left and assist Carter. But as there was still an interval between them, the regiment of cavalry which had come in on the left was transferred to the centre and ordered to make a strong skirmishing fight till Ruger's division could arrive on the ground. Palmer at the same time was ordered to demonstrate strongly toward the creek. Riding forward on the Dover road, I found Carter with the regiment from his division, still energetically striving to reach Upham. As the sound of the battle showed that the enemy was also in front of our centre, it was evident that we must make a concentration of our forces till the divisions were in touch with each other. I therefore directed Carter to make his main line in front of Wise's Forks as solid as possible, concentrating his artillery near the Dover road, and to limit the activity of the advanced regiment to bold skirmishing, drawing it back to the main line as the enemy advanced in force.

Hoke had evidently supposed that Upham's detachment on the British road was the flank of our principal position, and was surprised at finding strong demonstrations from the direction of Wise's Forks, now partly in his own rear. This checked his progress and made him turn upon Carter. The advanced regiment retired as ordered, and when it was within the lines the enemy was saluted with such a fire of artillery and musketry as instantly checked him. Although he repeated his efforts to force the position at the Forks several times, they all were futile, and Carter had at no time the least difficulty in holding his main line firmly.

In Palmer's division, when Hill's advance across the creek drove back the pickets and threatened to pass the left flank of Boughton's brigade, this officer drew back his left to the British road and threw up a hasty barricade there.[63] Claassen's brigade was sent to prolong Boughton's line to the left, and Ruger's division having come up, the connection between Palmer and Carter was secured, the latter advancing his brigades so as to

BGen. Thomas H. Ruger, USA

make a better continuous line. The attacks of Hoke and Hill extended across Ruger's front, but nothing heavier than brisk skirmishing occurred on Boughton's line. Claassen's brigade was sent forward toward Jackson's Mill, accompanied by my aide, Captain Tracy, in order to locate the left of the enemy's line, and determine the extent of his forces in front of our left and centre. No strong opposition was met till the Dover road came in sight, where the enemy were seen moving toward Hoke's position in front of Carter. Claassen was followed back in his orderly retirement to his position on Ruger's right, and was attacked there, but easily repulsed his assailants.[64]

Palmer had reported sharp skirmishing across his front all the way to the Neuse road on his right, and had drawn his lines back a little, so as to keep them in front of the British road, contracting his right and extending his left, as the sound of the fighting showed that the heaviest attacks were falling upon Carter. By the middle of the afternoon a continuous line of breastworks had been made along the whole of Palmer's division in front of the British road. Ruger had extended it diagonally till it joined Carter's right, the latter continuing it across the Dover road in front of Wise's Forks to a difficult swamp on the extreme left. For our left, the lower Trent road served for our communication along the front, and for our right the British road was used in like manner.

Late in the day there were indications of an attempt to turn Palmer's right on the Neuse road, and this, which added to the complexity of the situation, seems to have grown out of an excentric movement of the Confederate left under Hill. In crossing Southwest Creek to make his attack, he tells us the plan had been that when Hoke should strike our flank on the Dover road, he should cut off any retreat on the British and Neuse roads. This would be best accomplished by pushing straight from his bridges for the British road. But having made a circuit about a swamp to the rear of Upham's right, he received a note from Bragg's headquarters saying that Hoke wished he would enter the British road from the Neuse road, which implied a long circuit to their left. As Hoke had himself made the bridge by which Hill had crossed, and knew the field better than the rest by his skirmishes of the previous day, it is evident that there was an error in interpreting his wish. But as Hill was on ground unknown to him, and Bragg's dispatch directed Hoke's suggestion to be carried out, Hill obeyed, and turned his troops down the right bank of Southwest Creek, feeling the way to the Neuse road through swamps and woods. Reaching the outlet of the British road at half-past four without seeing signs of our retreat that way, and the distant firing showing that Hoke was not advancing, Hill thought it too late to venture further, and marched back by the way he had come five miles to his bridge.[65] His presence had been observed by our pickets and skirmishers, and was naturally interpreted by Palmer as the advance of a new column which had crossed the creek by the Neuse road. It, of course, gave an exaggerated impression of the enemy's strength, and as prisoners had been taken belonging to Lee's corps, who reported part of Hood's old army present with Bragg in command of the whole, we had to take into account the contingency of our having on our hands the formidable force thus indicated. Hill was met at his bridge by orders to cross to the left bank and join Hoke by recrossing at Jackson's Mills and following the Dover road. He effected the junction about midnight.[66] Hoke had been keeping up a skirmishing fight in the latter part of the day, and at night intrenched himself across the Dover road just in front of the British road. Hill, after joining him, continued the line northward, parallel to ours, and therefore crossing the British road again, recurving toward the creek. Our breastworks were made stronger, and we kept our teams hard at work bringing up ammunition and supplies. General Schofield went back to New Berne to get into communication with the rest of his department, and try to hurry forward the two old divisions of the Twenty-third Corps, who were marching to join us.[67] My own orders were to remain on the watchful defensive whilst the construction of the railroad toward us went on energetically.

On Thursday, the 9th, we husbanded our resources, for our ammunition was running short and the roads through the swamp were nearly impassable. We extended our works on Carter's left, recurving them so as to cross the lower Trent road, and, though we had no troops at the moment except one regiment of Ruger's to put into these intrenchments, they were ready for prompt occupation by any we might send there if another effort were made to turn that flank.[68] With this in view, General Ruger was directed to put one of his brigades in reserve, extending the rest of his troops to fill the vacancy so made, and covering the front with abatis and slashed timber. Pickets were advanced and every effort made to obtain information and keep close watch of the enemy's movements. About ten o'clock General Palmer reported a force moving toward the Neuse road which, after demonstrating there for some time, marched back again.[69] This seems to have been an effort to repeat the movement of Hill on the previous afternoon, but this time by Hoke's division. Finding Palmer's line in good earthworks, Hoke made no attack, and returned to his position, though Bragg's order declared that

Gen. George S. Greene, USA

"success must be achieved."[70] While this was going on, Hill advanced his line and drove in Carter's skirmishers; but these being reinforced, quickly retook their rifle-pits, and Hill retired to his own works.[71] Bragg's delay in testing conclusions with us was due, in part no doubt, to the fact that Stewart's corps of the Army of Tennessee was *en route* to him, and the railway was being worked energetically to bring up these reinforcements. They arrived during the day, and the final attack upon us was arranged for Friday, the 10th. Stewart's men were under the command of General Walthall, the senior division commander present.[72]

In the night of Thursday and the early morning of Friday, the active skirmishing of the enemy was so continuous as to remind us of the days in the Georgia campaign when the intrenched lines of the opposing armies faced each other in the narrow valley near New Hope Church.[73] Bragg ordered Hoke's troops to be relieved by Walthall's, and to make a considerable circuit to their right, seeking to reach the lower Trent road in our rear, and, advancing upon it, attack Carter's division in reverse. The sharp skirmishing had covered these changes of position. Upon hearing the sounds of Hoke's attack, Walthall and Hill were to assist him by strong demonstrations, but, as the latter says, in deference to his report that the men were very unwilling to attack earthworks, "their experience in the late campaign [in the west] not being favorable to such an undertaking," no actual assault was ordered, but doubled skirmish lines were to advance as far as possible.[74]

On our side we were watchful and expectant, my orders to the divisions being that whenever one part of the line should be engaged, the rest should push forward strong skirmish lines to test the extent of the enemy's deployment, and gain the information on which I could act in reinforcing either wing from the other. General Greene, who was on his way to rejoin Sherman, volunteered for duty as a staff officer,[75] as did General Stiles of my own division of the Twenty-third Corps, who was likewise returning to his proper command.[76] The absence of most of my own staff made their help most acceptable.

General Schofield was on his way up from New Berne, and horses were awaiting him at the end of the railway when, about half-past eleven, Hoke's attack came with much more energy and resolution than the Confederates had shown before. Ruger's reserve brigade (McQuiston's) was ordered over to the left at once, a brigade he had loaned to Palmer (Thomas's) was ordered back, and Palmer was ordered to send another brigade if the enemy was quiet in his front. Hoke's attack lapped so far over the lower Trent road as to threaten the Dover road also, and lest General Schofield should be in danger of capture, I directed Palmer to signal down the railroad track for him to await further news from us before leaving the train.[77]

The artillery of both Carter's and Ruger's divisions were concentrated upon Hoke, who was surprised to find our line so well prepared to meet him. For nearly an hour, however, the fighting was fierce; but it then began to flag a little, and I at once ordered McQuiston's brigade to charge, throwing the left forward upon Hoke's flank. This was decisive, and the enemy broke and fled. Walthall and Hill were now advancing against Carter's right and against Ruger, and as the line of the latter was very thin, I had to recall McQuiston in the full tide of pursuit and send him back to the centre double quick. He brought in nearly 300 prisoners, and our left was relieved of all danger. For a while my headquarters group was in a hot place. General Greene had his horse shot under him, one orderly had an arm taken off by a shell, two others were wounded, and several had horses killed.

The men of Stewart's and Lee's corps were to have co-operated with Hoke, but the difficulty of movement over such blind and wooded country caused delay which gave time for me to reinforce the centre. The artillery was hurried to the same position, and the Confederates were defeated easily, their unwillingness to assault breastworks being increased by the sight of Hoke's men in disordered flight. At half-past twelve I was able to send word to General Schofield that the road was no longer threatened by the enemy, and he joined us before the fighting at the centre was over.[78] Bragg withdrew to the intrenchments he had occupied on the 9th. The certainty that two corps of the Army of Tennessee were represented in the attack besides the troops of Bragg's own department, added to the lack of supplies and munitions, made us quite willing to remain on the defensive and await the arrival of Couch, who was within a day's march of us with the two veteran divisions of the Twenty-third Corps. The construction of the railroad and the hurrying forward of ammunition were ordered with strenuous urgency, and messages to Couch made him force the marching to join us.[79] Bragg retreated in the night of the 10th and was speeding back to Goldsborough by rail, for Johnston was now hastening to join Hardee, who was retreating before Sherman out of South Carolina.

The numbers which Hill and Walthall brought to Bragg were smaller than we inferred from our knowledge of the organizations present. We took prisoners belonging to four divisions of Hood's old army. Hoke's division and the brigades of Whitford, Hagood, and Baker had all been stronger in numbers than similar organizations of our own. We were necessarily wholly ignorant of the causes which had reduced the divisions coming from the West, and indeed learned of their presence in North Carolina only through the prisoners we took in the engagement and the deserters who came into our lines. As we have seen,[80] the number of Hood's men in the State at the beginning of the month was over 9000, with other detachments on the way. Bragg's other forces were an equal number. After all the casualties of the campaign, the Army of Tennessee reported 11,442 present on April 7th, of which 8953 were "effectives." When they were paroled at Greenesborough on April 26th, 17,934 appeared and signed the papers.[81] It is impossible to tell exactly what part of these were at Kinston. Hill's claim that he had but little over 1300 effectives in five brigades of Lee's corps is not credible.[82] It is certain that Bragg knew I had three divisions and that he believed his force was the stronger. Our losses had been 1337, of which 900 were the "missing" in Upton's brigade and the cavalry. Bragg made no formal report of the campaign or of his losses in this part of it.

Chapter XLVII Notes

1. Official Records, vol. xlvii. pt. ii. pp. 1202, 1204.

2. Official Records, vol. xlvii. pt. ii. pp. 1193, 1202, 1217, 1238.

3. *Id.*, pp. 1177, 1181, 1195, 1201-1202, 1204, 1223, 1258.

4. *Id.*, p. 1035.

5. *Id.*, p. 1016.

6. Official Records, vol. xlvii. pt. ii. p. 1189.

7. Lee to Vance, Id., p. 1270.

8. Official Records, vol. xlvii. pt. ii. pp. 1250-1255.

9. *Id.*, p. 1222.

10. Official Records, vol. xlvii. pt. ii. pp. 1229, 1237, 1238.

11. *Id.*, pt. i. p. 1.

12. *Id.*, pt. ii. p. 1247.

13. Official Records, vol. xlvii. pt. ii. pp. 1248, 1399.

14. *Id.*, p. 1047.

15. *Id.*, p. 1032.

16. *Id.*, vol. xlv. pt. i. p. 664. General Taylor volunteered to send the whole to Beauregard except French's division, which he said was very weak. Some Mississippi troops were given a short furlough, others took "French leave," and delays in transportation occurred, so that it is very hard to say how many of the Army of Tennessee were actually in the final combats in North Carolina. They all seem to have gathered there before the final surrender at Greensborough.

17. *Id.*, p. 1154.

18. *Id.*, p. 1084.

19. *Ibid.*

20. When Beauregard took command of the forces in South Carolina, etc., on February 16th, he reckoned them at "about 20,000 effective infantry and artillery, more or less demoralized," and said of Sherman's army that it numbered "nearly double our force." (Dispatch to Lee, Official Records, vol. xlvii. pt. ii. p. 1202.) This would make Sherman about 40,000 strong. Beauregard's underestimate of his own force is in accordance with the common habit of officers who are somewhat discouraged and wish to be reinforced.

21. *Id.*, p. 1084.

22. *Id.*, p. 1086.

23. *Id.*, p. 1238.

24. *Id.*, p. 1271. At the end of February, the portions of S. D. Lee's corps which had joined Beauregard had 2502 present for duty, Cheatham's 4697, Stewart's 1694, Engineers 185; total, 9078. (*Id.*, pp. 1285, 1326.) The rest of the Army of Tennessee were still in Georgia on their way to the front.

25. The complaints of marauding by Wheeler's cavalry had been loud and bitter, and inefficiency was charged. D. H. Hill to Hardee, Official Records, vol. xlvii. pt. ii. p. 1046; Do. to Iverson, pp. 1047, 1068; Beauregard to Lee, p. 1165; Davis to Hampton, 1207. For Wheeler's earnest defence, see *Id.*, pp. 987, 1004.
26. *Id.*, p. 1320.
27. *Id.*, p. 1328.
28. *Id.*, pp. 1002, 1003, 1272, 1317.
29. *Id.*, p. 1382.
30. See chap. li. *post.*
31. Official Records, vol. xlvii. pt. ii. pp. 305-306, 316-318, 501, 509, 561.
32. *Id.*, p. 559.
33. *Id.*, pp. 579, 580.
34. *Id.*, pt. i. pp. 930, 931.
35. *Id.*, pt. ii. pp. 581, 607, 620.
36. Official Records, vol. xlvii. pt. ii. pp. 607, 620, 637, 638.
38. *Id.*, pp. 157, 356, 384.
39. *Id.*, pp. 654, 683.
40. Official Records, vol. xlvii. pt. ii. p. 1318, 1329.
41. *Id.*, pp. 1334.
42. *Ibid.*
43. *Id.*, p. 1338.
44. Hill's Report, Official Records, vol. xlvii. pt. i. p. 1086.
45. *Id.*, pt. ii. p. 1339.
46. Official Records, vol. xlvii. pt. i. p. 1087.
47. *Id.*, pt. ii. pp. 654, 683.
48. *Id.*, pp. 706-708.
49. Official Records, vol. xlvii. pt. ii. p. 707.
50. Official Records, vol. xlvii. pt. ii. pp. 723-725.
51. *Id.*, pt. i. pp. 976, 981, 989.
52. *Id.*, pp. 993, 997.
53. Official Records, vol. xlvii. pt. i. p. 976.
54. *Ibid.*
55. Official Records, vol. xlvii. pt. ii. pp. 722-724.
56. *Id.*, pt i. p. 918.
57. *Id.*, pt. ii. p. 734.
58. Official Records, vol. xlvii. pt. ii. p. 734.
59. *Id.*, pt. i. pp. 977, 994.
60. *Ante*, pp. 429, 430.
61. Official Records, vol. xlvii. pt. i. pp. 997-999.
62. *Id.*, p. 1087.
63. Official Records, vol. xlvii. pt. i. p. 992.

64. Official Records, vol. xlvii. pt. i. pp. 982, 990.

65. Official Records, vol. xlvii. pt. i. p. 1087.

66. *Ibid*

67. Official Records, vol. xlvii. pt. ii. pp. 743-751.

68. *Id.*, pt. i. pp. 978, 995.

69. *Id.*, pt. ii. pp. 747, 749-750.

70. *Id.*, p. 1359.

71. Official Records, vol. xlvii. pt. i. p. 1087.

72. *Id.*, p. 1088.

73. *Id.*, pt. ii. p. 769.

74. *Id.*, pt. i. p. 1088.

75. Official Records, vol. xlvii. pt. i. p. 979.

76. General George S. Greene, division commander in the Twentieth Corps, had commanded a division in the Twelfth Corps, before its consolidation into the other. He was the same who was distinguished at Antietam (*ante*, vol. i. pp. 321-331). He graduated at West Point in 1823, and was a descendant of General Greene of the Revolutionary War, a military stock well continued in F. V. Greene of the Engineers, a general officer in the late Spanish War.

77. *Id.*, pt. ii. p. 772.

78. Official Records, vol. xlvii. pt. i. p. 978; pt. ii. p. 772.

79. The officer who was sent by Schofield to hasten Couch's march found my old division at the head of the column slowly filing over a rickety foot-bridge in the darkness, grumbling at the continued plodding in the mud. He shouted to them the news of our fighting and my possible need of help. The cry went up from the men, "If General Cox wants us, he can have us," and they dashed into the stream in solid column, forcing the pace till they reached the field.

80. *Ante*, p. 424.

81. Official Records, vol. xlvii. pt. i. pp. 1059, 1066. In the table of the paroled, Cheatham's two divisions (his own and Brown's) are listed in Hardee's corps, and with those of Stewart's and Lee's corps, less Anderson's (late Talliaferro's) division, make the total given.

82. [Footnote: *Id.*, p. 1088. For my criticism of his amusingly erroneous statements in regard to Antietam, see "The Nation," No. 1538, p. 462, and No. 1543, p. 71.

CHAPTER XLVIII

JUNCTION WITH SHERMAN AT GOLDSBOROUGH—THE MARCH ON RALEIGH—CESSATION OF HOSTILITIES

Occupation of Kinston—Opening of Neuse River—Rebel ram destroyed—
Listening to the distant battle at Bentonville—Entering Goldsborough—Meeting
Sherman—Grant's congratulations—His own plans—Sketch of Sherman's
march—Lee and Johnston's correspondence—Their gloomy outlook—Am made
commandant of Twenty-third Corps—Terry assigned to Tenth—Schofield
promoted in the Regular Army—Stanton's proviso—Ill effects of living on the
country—Stopping it in North Carolina—Camp jubilee over the fall of
Richmond—Changes in Sherman's plans—Our march on Smithfield—House-
burning—News of Lee's surrender—Overtures from Governor Vance—Entering
Raleigh—A mocking-bird's greeting—Further negotiations as to North
Carolina—Johnston proposes an armistice—Broader scope of negotiations—The
Southern people desire peace—Terrors of non-combatants assuaged—News of
Lincoln's assassination—Precautions to preserve order—The dawn of peace.

Reconnoitring parties sent toward Kinston on the 11th showed that only a
rear-guard occupied that town and that we could occupy it when we
pleased. General Couch joined us on the 12th, and Hoke having sent in a
flag of truce offering to exchange prisoners, of whom we had nearly 400, I sent
Major Dow of my staff with General Schofield's answer declining to do so. The
major found no enemy on our side of the Neuse. The railroad bridge was burned
and the middle part of the wagon bridge destroyed. The roads were so nearly
impassable that we could hardly feed the troops where we were, and whilst the
railroad building went on, we hastened also the opening of a supply line by

water.[1] Commander Rhind of the navy efficiently co-operated in this, and we marched to Kinston bridge on the 14th, laid pontoon bridges on the next day, and occupied the town. The Confederate ram had been burnt and her wreck lay a little below the bridge. The transports and their convoying war vessel did not get up till the 18th, but as they then brought a hundred thousand rations, we were able to begin accumulating stores at Kinston as an advanced depot.[2] Small additions to our wagon-trains also arrived, and orders were issued to march toward Goldsborough on the 20th. Meanwhile 2000 men had been set at work getting out railroad ties and timber for bridges.[3]

Cmdr. Alexander C. Rhind, USN

During the halt at Kinston we partly reorganized the troops in view of the approaching union with Sherman. The officers and men who belonged to the divisions in Sherman's army were separately organized into a division under General Greene, so that they could easily be transferred to their proper commands. The rest of Palmer's and Carter's divisions were united in one under Carter, and Palmer was assigned to the District of Beaufort, from which I was relieved. Ruger's division remained in my provisional corps with the other two. General Stiles was assigned to a brigade in Ruger's division.[4]

On Monday, the 20th, we were in march for Goldsborough, leaving a brigade to garrison the post at Kinston and protect the growing depot there. On Sunday we had heard all day the very distant artillery firing, which we knew indicated a battle between Sherman and Johnston. It was a scarcely distinguishable sound, like a dull thumping, becoming somewhat more distinct when one applied his ear to the ground. We judged that this final battle in the Carolinas was near Smithfield, and we were not far out of the way, for Bentonville was only a little south, and either place about fifty miles from us. Two days' march took us into Goldsborough with no opposition but skirmishing with the enemy's cavalry. We found the railroad uninjured, except that the bridges were burned; but they were small and would not delay Colonel Wright long when the large one at Kinston should be completed. Captain Twining, General Schofield's engineer and aide, had carried

The Battle of Bentonville.

dispatches to Sherman on the 20th, and the latter was now in full possession of the story of our movements since the fall of Fort Fisher.[5] On the 22d Sherman was able to announce in field orders the retreat of Johnston toward Raleigh and our occupation of Goldsborough, whilst Terry had laid his pontoons across the Neuse completing the connection with Wilmington also. His declaration for the whole army that the "campaign has resulted in a glorious success" was more than justified.[6]

On Thursday, the 23d, Sherman joined us in person, and we paraded the Twenty-third Corps to honor the march-past of Slocum's Army of Georgia, the Fourteenth and Twentieth Corps, as they came in from Bentonville. Sherman took his place with us by the roadside, and the formal reunion with the comrades who had fought with us in the Atlanta campaign was an event to stir deep emotions in our hearts. The general did not hesitate to speak out his readiness, now that his army was reunited, to meet the forces of Lee and Johnston combined, if they also should effect a junction and try to open a way southward. The men who had traversed the Carolinas were ragged and dirty, their faces were begrimed by the soot of their camp-fires of pine-knots in the forests, but their arms were in order, and they stepped out with the sturdy swing that marked all our Western troops. Our men were in new uniforms we had lately drawn from the quartermaster, and the tatterdemalions who had made the march to the sea were disposed to chaff us as if we were new recruits or pampered garrison troops. "Well, sonnies!" a regimental wag cried out, "do they issue butter to you regularly now?" "Oh, yes! to be sure!" was the instant retort; "but *we* trade it off for soap!" The ironical emphasis on the "we" was well understood and greeted with roars of laughter, and learning that our men were really those who had been with them in Georgia and had fought at Franklin and Nashville before making

Gen. H.W. Slocum, CSA

the tour of the North to come by sea and rejoin them in North Carolina, they made the welkin ring again with their greeting cheers.

Keeping close watch of Sherman's movements, as hinted at in the Southern newspapers,[7] Grant concluded on the 22d that he must have reached Goldsborough, and wrote him congratulations on the same day that Sherman announced to his army the good result. "I congratulate you and the army," said Grant, "in what may be regarded as the successful termination of the third campaign since leaving the Tennessee River less than one year ago."[8] He briefly but clearly outlined his own plans. Sheridan was to start with his cavalry on the 25th, and, passing beyond the left of the lines before Petersburg, to strike the Southside railroad as near the town as might be, and destroy enough of it to interrupt its use by the enemy for three or four days. This done, he was to push for the Danville Railroad, do the like, and again cut the Southside road near Burkesville. After that Grant would leave Sheridan at liberty to join Sherman or to return to his own army. At the same time he would himself diminish the forces in his investing lines to the smallest that could hold them, and with all the rest crowd to the westward to prevent Lee from following Sheridan. He would attack if Lee should detach part of his army to follow Sheridan or to join Johnston, or would fight a decisive battle if the Confederates came out in force.[9] The general principles which resulted in Five Forks and the abandonment of Richmond are here clearly evident, and Sherman could plan his own work accordingly.

The latter was also writing on that day to the Lieutenant-General, taking up the thread of his own story from the time he reached Fayetteville and learned that Johnston had been put in command of all the forces opposing him. He sketched the sharp combat between Slocum and Hardee at Averasborough on March 16th, where the latter had taken a strong position across the narrow swampy neck between Cape Fear River and North River at the forks of the

Raleigh and Goldsborough roads. Hardee was working for time, as Johnston was collecting his forces at Smithfield after Bragg's unsuccessful blow at us near Kinston. A day's delay was gained at heavy cost for the Confederates. At Bentonville, on the 19th, Johnston had concentrated his army and struck fiercely at Slocum again, for the almost impassable mud had made it necessary for Howard's wing to seek roads some miles to the right. Slocum had to give some ground and draw back his advanced division to a better position, on which he formed the rest of his troops, Kilpatrick's cavalry covering his left. Here he repulsed all further efforts of Johnston and held his ground till Sherman could bring forward the right wing, when the enemy was forced to intrench and was put on the defensive. On the 21st Howard's extreme right broke through or turned the line, and nearly reached Johnston's headquarters. The blindly tangled swampy ground prevented full advantage being reaped from this success, and Johnston managed to hold on till night, when he abandoned his lines and retreated on Raleigh. Sherman's casualties of all sorts in the two engagements of Averasborough and Bentonville were 2209. He had buried on the abandoned fields 375 of the Confederate dead, and held 2000 prisoners. Johnston's wounded were 1694 at Bentonville, besides several hundred at Averasborough.[10] The last battle in the Carolinas had been fought, Johnston had added to his reputation as a soldier by quick and strong blows skilfully delivered, first at Schofield, then at Sherman; but his numbers were not enough to make either blow successful, and the junction of our armies at Goldsborough made further fighting a mere waste of life, unless he and Lee could unite for a final effort. This Grant would not permit, and Johnston's message to Lee on the 23d was in substance the old one from Pavia, "All is lost but honor." "Sherman's course cannot be hindered by the small force I have. I can do no more than annoy him. I respectfully suggest that it is no longer a question whether you leave your present position; you have only to decide where to meet Sherman. I will be near him."[11]

General Lee, from his own point of view, saw with equal clearness the net that was closing round him. He had telegraphed to Johnston on the 11th, "I

The Battle of Averasboro.

fear I cannot hold my position if road to Raleigh is interrupted. Should you be forced back in this direction both armies would certainly starve."[12] On the 15th he repeated, "If you are forced back from Raleigh and we deprived of the supplies from east North Carolina, I do not know how this army can be supported."[13] But while he pointed out the vital importance of repulsing Sherman, he did not urge rashness in giving battle without prospect of success. Supplies in Virginia, he said, were exhausted. The western communication by Danville was now his only reliance. Since sending Hoke, Conner, and Hampton south, his forces were too weak to extend his lines, and he apprehended the very break in the Danville road which Grant was planning to make by Sheridan. "You will therefore perceive," he added, "that if I contract my lines as you propose, with the view of holding Richmond, our only resource for obtaining subsistence will be cut off and the city must be abandoned; whereas, if I take a position to maintain the road, Richmond will be lost." If Sherman could not be checked, "I cannot remain here, but must start out and seek a favorable opportunity for battle. I shall maintain my position as long as it appears advisable, both from the moral and material advantages of holding Richmond and Virginia."[14] Danville, he saw, was his necessary aim if he broke away, and he pointed out the advantages they would have for manoeuvre if Sherman could be kept well to the east, giving them more room and a wider region to live upon after uniting. But Grant saw all this too, and the inexorable tenacity and vigor with which, a few days later, he pushed Lee north of the Danville line and cornered him at Appomattox, showed that his measure of the situation was as accurate as Lee's, and that he knew the quick ending of the war depended on his preventing at all hazards the junction of the Confederate armies. Nothing in military history is more interesting than the comparison of the letters and dispatches of the leaders on both sides in this crisis. Grant was not content with being upon Lee's heels when he abandoned Richmond, as he had promised Sherman he would be. He would do better. Well served by Sheridan's fiery energy, he would out-foot his adversary in the race for Danville, and even block his path on the road to Lynchburg when the junction with Johnston had to be given up.

For us at Goldsborough a day or two was delightfully spent in free conferences with Sherman and in getting from his own lips the story of his wonderful campaigns since we parted from him in Georgia. All the empty wagons of his enormous trains were now sent back to Kinston under escort to bring up clothing and supplies, and he thought a delay of a fortnight might be necessary to get ready for further active movements. He fixed April both as the date for opening a new campaign, and suggested to General Grant that when he had his troops properly placed and the supplies working well, he might "run up and see you for a day or two before diving again into the bowels of the country."[25] On the 25th the railroad was running to Goldsborough, and Colonel

Wright was anxious to have the general go over the road with him and see for himself its condition and what had been acomplished as well as what was still needed to make its equipment ready for the heavy work of another campaign. Accordingly Sherman put Schofield temporarily in chief command, and after an inspection trip on a locomotive with Colonel Wright, he continued his journey to City Point in a steamer belonging to the quartermaster's department.[16] His memorable visit to Grant and Lincoln, there, will be considered in connection with the negotiations with Johnston a little later. Having spent the 27th and 28th of March there, he was sent back by Admiral Porter in a fast vessel of the navy, reached New Berne on the 30th, and rejoined us at Goldsborough the same evening.

His return was a matter of some personal interest to me, for it brought my permanent assignment to the command of the Twenty-third Corps by Presidential order. The other troops under Schofield were organized into a new corps with Terry for commandant, and as changes had vacated the original Tenth Corps organization, that number was given to Terry's. Schofield had asked for these appointments immediately after our occupation of Wilmington, but the letters had not reached General Grant, and action had not been taken.[17] At Goldsborough he had renewed the request which Sherman cordially indorsed, and the latter carried the papers with him to City Point, where the matter was acted upon at once by the President and General Grant.[18]

Schofield's promotion to the rank of brigadier-general in the regular army had been recommended by Grant as a reward for the capture of Wilmington, with the remark that he ought to have had it from the battle of Franklin.[19] Mr. Stanton replied that the nomination would be made as requested, "subject, however, to his obedience to orders. I am not satisfied with his conduct in seizing the hospital boat 'Spaulding' to make it his own quarters," he said; adding, "I have directed him to give it up. If he obeys the order promptly, I will send in his nomination; otherwise I will not."[20] By an odd coincidence, the order to Schofield with the Secretary's reprimand was written on the same day Grant was making his recommendation for promotion,[21] and it well illustrates Stanton's characteristic impulsiveness and hasty temper which made him act on first reports, when a quiet investigation of facts would have changed his view and saved the feelings of his subordinates. An order forbidding the use of hospital boats for other military purposes, diverting them from hospital use, had been issued on February 8th, the day we reached Cape Fear Inlet after our sea voyage,[22] and by another coincidence Schofield had made the "Spaulding" his temporary headquarters on the same day.[23] Not being a clairvoyant, Schofield knew nothing of the order which was then being written in the adjutant-general's office at Washington, and which did not reach him till his temporary use of the vessel had ended. Moreover, as he was as yet without his tents or horses, and as he intended his troops to operate on both sides of Cape Fear River, his prompt progress with the campaign depended on his ready communication with both banks,[24] and the boat had been named as available for the purpose by the quartermaster responsible for the army transports and vessels.

As it was a question of successful handling of his forces, the discretion would have belonged to the general commanding the department to make an exception to a rule, if the order had been in his hands instead of being wholly unknown to him. Still again, the use he made of the boat helped instead of hindering its availability as a hospital, for he kept it close to the advancing lines on the river banks so that the wounded were brought to it with greatest ease, and it had in fact no sick or disabled men on board till they were brought there under these circumstances. Lastly, the superior medical officer of the department was a member of Schofield's staff, wholly in accord with his views, and the complaint had been sent by the subordinate surgeon on the boat directly to the surgeon-general at Washington without the knowledge of the department medical director. To have referred it back to the general for his comments, calling his attention to the order, would have been regular and would have resulted in commendation of his action instead of disapproval. When Grant received the Secretary's dispatch, Colonel Comstock had returned from Wilmington, and from him the general got the information which enabled him to remove Stanton's misapprehension, so that the appointment was made before Schofield knew of the complaint.[25] Nearly a month later he made a full statement of the circumstances to put himself personally right with the Secretary.[26] The latter had borne no ill-will to Schofield, but even at the closing period of the war had not learned to temper his zeal with considerate patience.

The work which occupied us the ten days of April which we spent at Goldsborough was chiefly that of organizing our trains and collecting supplies in our depots, so that the foraging on the country which had been necessary in Georgia and South Carolina might cease, now that we had railway communication with a safe base on the Atlantic. Sherman had informed his principal subordinates that when he reached North Carolina he would resume the regular issue of supplies as far as possible, and put an end to the indiscriminate seizing of whatever the army needed. It had answered its purpose in the long marches from Atlanta to Savannah and from Savannah to Goldsborough, where the condition of success was cutting loose from the base; but the tendency to demoralization and loss of discipline in troops which practise it too long, made a return to regular methods very desirable.

As the army had approached the North Carolina line, General Blair, commanding the Seventeenth Corps, had written to Howard, his immediate superior: "Every house that we pass is pillaged, and as we are about to enter the State of North Carolina, I think the people should be treated more considerately.

The only way to prevent this state of affairs is to put a stop to foraging. I have enough in my wagons to last to Goldsborough, and I suppose that the rest of the army has also. . . . The system is vicious and its results utterly deplorable. As there is no longer a necessity for it, I beg that an order may be issued to prohibit it. General Sherman said that when we reached North Carolina he would pay for everything brought to us and forbid foraging. I believe it would have an excellent effect upon the country to change our policy in this respect."[27] Stringent orders were at once issued to modify the system and prevent the abuses of it, but it was not practicable to stop foraging entirely till the junction of the forces was made at Goldsborough.[28] The regular issue of rations furnished by the government was then resumed, except that long forage for horses and mules could not be obtained in this way and was collected from the country;[29] but even then the correction of bad habits in the soldiery was only gradually accomplished.

The evacuation of Richmond and Petersburg on the morning of the 3d of April was not known to Sherman till the 6th, when Grant's letter reached him containing the joyful news. On Saturday, the 8th, it was confirmed, with particulars of Lee's disastrous retreat.[30] That night there was a noisy jubilee in our camps. Regular artillery salutes were fired, but the soldiers also extemporized all sorts of demonstrations of their joyfulness. The air resounded with cheers, with patriotic songs, with the beating of drums, with the music of the brass bands, with musket firing; whilst beautiful signal rockets rushed high into the air, dropping their brilliant stars of red, white, and blue from the very clouds.[31]

So long as Lee held fast at Petersburg, Sherman's plan had been to feint on Raleigh, but make his real movement northward, crossing the Roanoke above Gaston and marching between Johnston and Lee.[32] Now, however, as he wrote Halleck, he would move in force upon Raleigh, repairing the railroad behind him and following the Confederate army close in whatever direction it should move.[33] Grant's letter of the 5th, giving his opinion that Lee was making for Danville with an army reduced to about 20,000 men,[34] reached Sherman on the 8th, and he immediately answered it, saying: "On Monday [10th] all my army will move straight on Joe Johnston, supposed to be between me and Raleigh, and I will follow him wherever he may go. If he retreats on Danville to make junction with Lee, I will do the same, though I may take a course round him, bending toward Greensborough for the purpose of turning him north.... I wish you could have waited a few days or that I could have been here a week sooner; but it is not too late yet, and you may rely with absolute certainty that I will be after Johnston with about 80,000 men, provided for twenty full days which will last me forty. I will have a small force here at Goldsborough and will repair the road to Raleigh."[35]

On Monday we marched,—Slocum with the Army of Georgia straight
for Smithfield, Howard with the Army of the Tennessee going north to Pikeville
and then turning toward Raleigh, keeping to the right of Slocum and abreast of
him on parallel roads. Schofield with our Army of the Ohio moved a little to the
left of Slocum in echelon, my corps taking the river road on the left (north) bank
of the Neuse to Turner's Bridge, a little below Smithfield, and Terry's going
through Bentonville somewhat further to left and rear. Kilpatrick with the
cavalry covered the march of this flank.[36] It will be seen that this order of
movement assumed that Johnston was at or near Smithfield, where our latest
information put him. My corps had been somewhat scattered to cover our
communications with Kinston and Newberne, and I was ordered to concentrate
at Goldsborough on the 10th, advancing-from there on the 11th.[37] My old
division, which had been commanded by General Reilly since he joined us at
Wilmington, was for the rest of the campaign led by General Carter, Reilly's
uncertain health making him anticipate the quickly approaching end of the war
by resigning. Ruger and Couch continued in command of the first and second
divisions respectively.[38]

My own march was impeded by the slow progress of the pontoon-train
which had been sent ahead of my column, where a part of Slocum's supply-train
also moved. For this reason we found numbers of stragglers on our way and
evidences of pillaging by which I was exasperated. We halted at noon of the 11th
near a large house belonging to a Mr. Atkinson, a man of prominence in the
region. The mansion had a Grecian portico with large columns the whole height
of the building. Part of the furniture and the carpets had been removed, but
evidences of refinement and intelligence were seen in the piano and the library
with its books. With my staff I rested and ate my lunch in the spacious portico,
and moving on when the halt was over, I had hardly ridden half a mile when a
pillar of white smoke showed that the house was on fire. I sent back a staff
officer in haste to order an instant investigation and the arrest of any authors of
this vandalism. The most that could be learned was that some stragglers of
another corps had been seen lurking in the house when we moved on, and soon
after fire broke out in the second story, having been set, apparently, in a closet
connected with one of the chambers. Efforts were made to extinguish it, but it
had found its way into the garret and had such headway that the house was
doomed.[39] This was the first instance in my experience where a dwelling had
been burned when my troops were passing, and I was greatly disturbed by their
apparent responsibility for it. My anger was increased by repetitions of similar
outrages during the afternoon. From our camp at Turner's Bridge I issued an
order directing summary trial by drum-head court-martial and execution of
marauders guilty of such outrages, whether belonging to my own corps or
stragglers hanging on at its skirts.[40] The evidence seemed conclusive that the

"Bummers" pillaged across the North Carolina countryside in the wake of the army.

crimes were committed by "bummers" who had separated themselves from the army when marching up from Savannah, and were following it for purposes of pillage.[41] It was reported that Atkinson was a "conscription agent" of the Confederate government, and this perhaps was the incentive in his case for the outrage. As a precaution, I ordered sentinels to be left at dwellings on our march, to be relieved from the divisions in succession, the last to remain till our trains had passed and then join the rear-guard.[42]

In the march of the 12th Howard remained on the east side of the Neuse with a pretty widely extended front, aiming for the crossing of the river due east of Raleigh, at the Neuse Mills and Hinton's Bridge. Slocum crossed at Smithfield and took the roads up the right bank of the Neuse. Schofield crossed at Turner's Bridge, and sought roads further west, intending to reach the main road leading from Elevation to Raleigh.[43] At Smithfield we learned that Johnston was at Raleigh, but we did not know that he had heard of Lee's surrender and had no longer a motive to hold tenaciously to the central part of the State.[44]

It was on our march of Tuesday, the 12th, that the news of the surrender reached us, and was greeted with extravagant demonstrations of joy by both officers and men.[45] Sherman had got the news in a dispatch sent by Grant on the 9th, as soon as the capitulation was complete, and which contained the terms he had offered Lee, with their acceptance.[46] Replying at once, Sherman said, "I hardly know how to express my feelings, but you can imagine them. The terms

Lee's surrender at Appomatox was the death knell for the Confederates in N.C.

you have given Lee are magnanimous and liberal. Should Johnston follow Lee's example, I shall of course grant the same. He is retreating before me on Raleigh, but I shall be there to-morrow."[47] He indicated his hope that Johnston would surrender at Raleigh, but should he not do so, his own plan would be to push to the south and west to prevent the enemy's retreat into the Gulf States. "With a little more cavalry," he said, "I would be sure to capture the whole army." He issued also a Special Field Order, announcing to the army the momentous news. "Glory to God and to our country, and all honor to our comrades in arms toward whom we are marching. A little more labor, a little more toil on our part, the great race is won, and our government stands regenerated after four years of bloody war."[48] Such were the words which created a tumult of emotion in the heart of every soldier, when they were read that day, a beautiful spring day, at the head of each command. The order reached me near mid-day at a resting halt of the corps, and with bared heads my staff listened to the reading. We then greeted it with three cheers, I myself acting as fugleman, and the tidings sped down the column on the wings of the wind.

Late in the same day a delegation met Slocum's advance-guard coming from Raleigh in a car upon the railroad with a letter from Governor Vance making overtures to end the war, so far as North Carolina was concerned. The little party was headed by ex-Governor Graham and Mr. Swain, men who had led the opposition to secession till swept away by the popular whirlwind of war feeling, and who now came to acknowledge the victory of the National Government. Mr. Graham had been the candidate for Vice-President in 1852, nominated by the Whig party on the ticket with General Scott. Sherman received them kindly, and gave a safeguard for Governor Vance and any members of the State government who might await him in Raleigh, though, after a conference with Graham and his party in regard to their present relations to the Confederate government, he wrote to Vance, "I doubt if hostilities can be suspended as between the Army of the Confederate Government and the one I command, but I will aid you all in my power to contribute to the end you aim to reach, the termination of the existing war."[49]

Gov. Zebulon Vance

The Twenty-third Corps marched eighteen miles on the 12th, and, as General Schofield reported, found that "Slocum's bummers had been all over the country," foraging it bare.[50] On the 13th we marched within two miles of Raleigh, making nineteen miles, the Army of Georgia entering the city just ahead of us. Sherman was with the head of Slocum's column, expecting to meet Governor Vance, but such delays had occurred to the train taking his messengers that Vance lost confidence, and had left the city ahead of Hampton's cavalry, the rear-guard of Johnston's army. Hampton was bitterly opposed to all negotiation by Vance, holding it to be treasonable, and had put such obstacles in the way of Graham's party as to make Vance think that they had been arrested and that the mission had failed.[51] Graham and Swain, however, were still there, and at once waited upon Sherman, who established his headquarters in the governor's mansion. The news, as it came to us in the marching column, was that Vance had met Sherman in person and surrendered the capital of the State; but the facts turned out to be as I have stated them.[52]

Ex-Gov. William Graham

A trifling incident gave us pleasure as we were approaching our camp near Raleigh, and, with the soldiers' disposition to interpret fortuitous things in earth and air, was greeted as a good omen.

David L. Swain

A great tree stood at the roadside, and, perched upon a dead limb high above the foliage and overhanging the way, a mocking-bird poured forth the most wonderful melodies ever heard even from that prince of songsters. Excited but not frightened away by the moving host beneath, the bird outdid its kind in its imitations of other birds, and in its calls and notes of endless variety, whistling and singing with a full resonant power that rose above all other sounds. The marching soldiers ceased their talk, listening intently and craning their necks to get a sight of the peerless musician. It was a celebration of the coming peace, unique in beauty and full of sweet suggestions.

On the 14th the greater part of the army moved westward a few miles in front of Raleigh, the Twenty-third Corps closing up to the eastern suburbs of the town. Sherman issued his marching orders for the 15th, beginning, "The next movement will be on Ashborough, to turn the position of the enemy at Company's shops in rear of Haw River Bridge and at Greensborough, and to cut off his only available line of retreat by Salisbury and Charlotte."[53] This march had hardly begun, however, when it was temporarily suspended and was never resumed. Our last hostile march against the Confederate armies had been made. Mr. Badger, the last senator from the State in the National Congress, and other leading men, including Mr. Holden, the leader of the Union element in the State, had joined Mr. Graham's party, and Sherman had been busy with them, negotiating informally to obtain the withdrawal of North Carolina from the Confederacy. The general was willing that the executive and legislature of the State should come to Raleigh for this purpose, but refused to suspend hostilities against Johnston's army except upon direct overtures for surrender on the part of the latter.[54] Whilst these conferences were in progress, others had been going on at Greensborough, and as a result General Johnston had sent a letter requesting an armistice.[55] Sherman immediately replied in terms which brought about the halt and temporary truce between the two armies and a personal conference three days later. Thus opened the famous negotiations, the story of which will be told in the next chapter.

Whilst the Southern people had shown wonderful fortitude and patience as long as a hope of success remained, they were most anxious to be spared the horrors of war when there was no compensating advantage to be looked for. The dread of our armies had been increased by the exaggerations which the Confederate authorities had used to excite the people to desperate resistance, and the terror now reacted in a general popular demand for surrender. The story of the burning of Columbia had been given to them as a wanton and deliberate barbarity on Sherman's part, and the delegation which met him could hardly believe their own senses when they heard his earnest expressions of desire to end the war at once and save the people from suffering and the country from devastation.

An experience of my own as we entered Raleigh gave me a startling view of the abject terror which had seized upon helpless families when they found themselves defenceless in our hands. In the night of Wednesday, the 12th, Hampton had made it known that the rear-guard which he commanded must retire before daylight, and the frightened people had at once begun to close their windows and sit in gloomy expectation of what the morning would bring. Early on Thursday Kilpatrick's cavalry clattered through the town, and on the further side some skirmishing occurred and an occasional cannon shot was thought to be the opening of battle. Slocum's infantry marched through after the cavalry advance-guard, and the heavy rattling of cannon and caissons with the shouting of the drivers of the trains seemed a pandemonium to unaccustomed ears.

Sherman had issued stringent orders that no mischief should be done and no looting permitted in the city, and all the superior officers were earnest in enforcing the orders, so that I believe no town was ever more quietly occupied by an army in actual war.

Gen. Kilpatrick, USA

On Friday morning I was placing my own troops in the suburb and arranging to assume the guard of the city, left to us by the camping of the main body of the army beyond its western limits. An officer of the general staff came to me, saying he had been appealed to in a most piteous way for protection by a lady who with her household of women and children could endure the terror and suspense no longer. Knowing that I was to be in immediate charge of the place, he had given assurances that I would remove all cause for fear, but had still been begged to ask me to come in person and relieve their great distress. I went with him to one of the most comfortable homes of the town. The family had been collected in the parlors since midnight of Wednesday. They had not dared to retire to sleep, but clung about the mother and mistress. The windows were close shut, the rooms lit by candles, and pale, jaded with the long nervous strain, momentarily fearing the breaking in of those they had been taught to look upon as little better than fiends, their hollow eyes showed they were perilously near the limit of human endurance. I earnestly vouched for the good intentions of our generals, and promised the most ample protection. I assured them of sympathy and a purpose to give them the same safety as I should wish for my own wife and children if they were in a like situation. A guard was ordered for the house and the neighborhood. They were urged to open the windows to the cheerful light and to resume their ordinary way of life. The passing of the panic

Lincoln's assassination nearly scuttled surrender negotiations in Raleigh.

and the revival of confidence was a sort of return from the shadow of death and was most touching to behold. It added a new element of thankfulness that such terrors for the helpless were not to be renewed, since peace was really coming to heal the terrible wounds of war.

There was a moment when we once more feared we might not be able to save the city from vengeance. It was when, on the 17th of April, the news of Lincoln's assassination reached us.[56] Sherman had received the dispatch in cipher just as he was starting for his conference with Johnston at Durham Station, and had enjoined absolute secrecy upon the telegraph operator till his return in the evening. General Stiles, one of my most trusted subordinates, had been made commandant of the post of Raleigh with a garrison of three battalions of infantry, a brigade of reserve artillery, and the convalescents of the Army of the Ohio.[57] As soon as Sherman returned from his visit to Johnston, he sent for me and told me the terrible news of Lincoln's murder. He expressed the great fear he had lest, on its becoming known, it should be the occasion of outbreaks among the soldiers. He charged me to strengthen Stiles's garrison to any extent I might think necessary, to put strong guards at the edge of the city on the roads leading to the several camps, to send all soldiers off duty to their proper commands, and in short, till the first excitement should be over, to allow no one to visit the city or wander about it, and to keep all under strict military surveillance. Schofield and the other army commanders were with him, and all were seriously impressed with the danger of mischief resulting and with the need of thorough precautions. Sherman's general order announcing the assassination was then read, but its distribution and publication to the army was delayed till I should have time to prepare for safeguarding the city.[58] Fortunately the announcement of the first convention for the disbanding of all the remaining armies of the Confederacy accompanied the exciting news, and as it was regarded as the return of general peace, the effect on our army was that of deep mourning for the loss of a great leader in the hour of victory rather than an excitement to vengeance in a continuing strife. There was no noteworthy difficulty in preserving order, and, though the inhabitants of Raleigh had a day or two of great uneasiness, the beautiful town did not suffer in the least. Its broad streets, lined with forest trees, and the ample dooryards in the lush beauty of lawns and flowers were no more trespassed upon than the avenues and gardens of Washington, and nobody suffered from violence.

Chapter XLVIII

1. Official Records, vol. xlvii. pt. i. pp. 933, 934; pt. ii. pp. 801, 802, 814.
2. Official Records, vol. xlvii. pt. ii. pp. 836-839, 880, 883.
3. *Id.*, pp. 836, 851.
4. *Id.*, pp. 839, 895.
5. Official Records, vol. xlvii. pt. ii. p. 942.
6. *Id.*, pt. i. p. 44.
7. Till the capture of Columbia, the Southern newspapers gave Sherman's movements with satisfactory accuracy, and Grant's information on the subject was chiefly drawn from them. Afterward a more rigid censorship was enforced. Official Records, vol. xlvii. pt. ii. pp. 385, 405, 428, 441, 455, 472, 499, etc.
8. *Id.*, p. 948.
9. Official Records, vol. xlvii. pt. ii. p. 948. See also p. 859.
10. Sherman to Grant, Official Records, vol. xlvii. pt. ii. p. 949; his report, Id., pt. i. pp. 27, 66, 76; Johnston's do., Id., pp. 1057, 1060.
11. *Id.*, p. 1055.
12. *Id.*, pt. ii. p. 1372.
13. *Id.*, p. 1395.
14. Official Records, vol. xlvii. pt. ii. p. 1395.
15. Official Records, vol. xlvii. pt. ii. p. 969.

16. *Id.*, pt. iii. pp. 19, 20.
17. Official Records, vol. xlvii. pt. ii. p. 559.
18. *Id.*, pp. 960, 961; pt. iii. pp. 18, 34.
19. *Id.*, pt. ii. pp. 545, 558.
20. *Id.*, p. 562.
21. *Id.*, p. 545.
22. *Id.*, p. 342.
23. *Id.*, pt. i. p. 927.
24. *Ante*, p. 405.
25. Official Records, vol. xlvii. pt. ii. pp. 562, 582.
26. *Id.*, p. 832.
27. Official Records, vol. xlvii. pt. ii. p. 717; pt. iii. pp. 46, 47.
28. Official Records, vol. xlvii. pt. ii. pp. 718, 728, 760, 783.
29. *Id.*, pt. iii. pp. 7-9.
30. *Id.*, pp. 89, 99, 100.
31. *Id.*, pt. i. p. 936.
32. *Id.*, pt. iii. p. 102.
33. *Id.*, p. 118.
34. *Id.*, P. 99.
35. Official Records, vol. xlvii. pt. iii. p. 129.
36. [*Id.*, p. 123.
37. *Id.*, p. 134.
38. *Id.*, pt. i. p. 936.
39. Official Records, vol. xlvii. pt. i. p. 936.
40. *Id.*, pt. iii. p. 189.
41. Official Records, vol. xlvii. pt. iii. p. 281.
42. *Id.*, p. 189.
43. *Id.*, pp. 163, 164, 187-189.
44. *Id.*, p. 777.
45. For a vivid description of the scene, see "Ohio Loyal Legion Papers," vol. ii. p. 234, by A. J. Ricks, then a lieutenant on my staff, since Judge of U. S. District Court, N. Ohio.
46. Official Records, vol. xlvii. pt. iii. p. 140.
47. Official Records, vol. xlvii. pt. iii. p. 177.
48. *Id.*, p. 180.
49. Official Records, vol. xlvii. pt. iii. p. 178.
50. *Id.*, p. 187.
51. *Id.*, pp. 178, 196.
52. *Id.*, pt. i. p. 937.
53. Official Records, vol. xlvii. pt. iii. pp. 208, 217.
54. *Id.*, p. 221.

55. *Id.*, p. 206.
56. Official Records, vol. xlvii. pt. iii. p. 221.
57. *Id.*, p. 217.
58. *Id.*, p. 238.

CHAPTER XLIX

THE SHERMAN-JOHNSTON CONVENTION

Sherman's earlier views of the slavery question—Opinions in 1864—War rights vs. statesmanship—Correspondence with Halleck—Conference with Stanton at Savannah—Letter to General Robert Anderson—Conference with Lincoln at City Point—First effect of the assassination of the President—Situation on the Confederate side—Davis at Danville—Cut off from Lee—Goes to Greensborough—Calls Johnston to conference—Lee's surrender—The Greensborough meeting—Approach of Stoneman's cavalry raid—Vance's deputation to Sherman—Davis orders their arrest—Vance asserts his loyalty—Attempts to concentrate Confederate forces on the Greensborough-Charlotte line—Cabinet meeting—Overthrow of the Confederacy acknowledged—Davis still hopeful—Yields to the cabinet—Dictates Johnston's letter to Sherman—Sherman's reply—Meeting arranged—Sherman sends preliminary correspondence to Washington—The Durham meeting—The negotiations—Two points of difficulty—Second day's session—Johnston's power to promise the disbanding of the civil government—The terms agreed upon—Transmittal letters—Assembling the Virginia legislature—Sherman's wish to make explicit declaration of the end of slavery—The assassination affecting public sentiment—Sherman's personal faith in Johnston—He sees the need of modifying the terms—Grant's arrival.

To understand Sherman's negotiations with Johnston, we must recall the general's attitude toward the rebellious States and his views on the subject of slavery. Originally a conservative Whig in politics, deprecating the anti-slavery agitation, as early as 1856 he had written to his brother, "Unless people both North and South learn more moderation, we'll 'see sights' in the way of civil war. Of course the North have the strength and must prevail, though the people of the South could and would be desperate enough."[1] In 1859 he was still urging concessions instead of insisting on the absolute right, saying, "Each State has a perfect right to have its own local policy, and a majority in Congress has an absolute right to govern the whole country; but the North, being so strong in every sense of the term, can well afford to be generous, even to making reasonable concessions to the weakness and prejudices of the South."[2] He returned to the same thought in 1860, saying, "So certain and inevitable is it that the physical and political power of this nation must pass into the hands of the free States, that I think you all can well afford to take things easy, bear the

Thaddeus Stevens

buffets of a sinking dynasty, and even smile at their impotent threats."[3]

The world is familiar with the ringing words with which he threw away his livelihood and turned from every attractive outlook in life, when, Secession having actually come, he said to the governor of Louisiana, "On no earthly account will I do any act or think any thought hostile to or in defiance of the United States."[4] But he was also one of the clearest-sighted in seeing that when slavery had appealed to the sword it would perish by the sword. In January, 1864, he expressed it tersely: "The South has made the interests of slavery the issue of the war. If they lose the war, they lose slavery."[5] At the end of the same month he said, "Three years ago, by a little reflection and patience, they could have had a hundred years of peace and prosperity; but they

preferred war. Last year they could have saved their slaves, but now it is too late,—all the powers of earth cannot restore to them their slaves any more than their dead grandfathers."[6] And in the same letter, written to a subordinate with express authority to make it known to the Southern people within our lines, he said of certain administrative regulations: "These are well-established principles of war, and the people of the South, having appealed to war, are barred from appealing for protection to our Constitution, which they have practically and publicly defied. They have appealed to war, and must abide *its* rules and laws."[7]

Two years later Thaddeus Stevens, as radical leader in Congress, enounced the same doctrine in no more trenchant terms. Sherman was explicit in regard to its scope, but he differed from Stevens in the extent to which he would go, as a matter of sound policy and statesmanship, in applying the possible penalties of war when submission was made. It is clear that he insisted there could be no resurrection for slavery, and that the freedmen must be protected in life, liberty, and property, with a true equality before the law in this protection; but he held that they were as yet unfit for political participation in the government, much less for the assumption of political rule in the Southern States.

In a friendly letter which General Halleck wrote to Sherman immediately after the capture of Savannah, he said with a freedom that long intimacy permitted: "Whilst almost every one is praising your great march through Georgia and the capture of Savannah, there is a certain class, having now great influence with the President and very probably anticipating still more on a change of cabinet, who are decidedly disposed to make a point against you—I mean in regard to 'Inevitable Sambo.' They say that you have manifested an almost *criminal* dislike to the negro, and that you are not willing to carry out the wishes of the government in regard to him, but repulse him with contempt."[8] In short, it was said that his march through Georgia might have been made the means of a general exodus of the slaves, and ought to have been.

Sherman made a humorous reply, saying he allowed thousands of negroes to accompany his march, and set no limit but the necessities of his military operations. "If it be insisted," he said, "that I shall so conduct my operations that the negro alone is consulted, of course I will be defeated, and then where will be Sambo? Don't military success imply the safety of Sambo, and *vice versa*?... They gather round me in crowds, and I can't find out whether I am Moses or Aaron or which of the prophets. . . . The South deserves all she has got for her injustice to the negro, but that is no reason why we should go to the other extreme. I do and will do the best I can for negroes, and feel sure that the problem is solving itself slowly and naturally. It needs nothing more than our fostering care."[9]

The Secretary of War was broadly hinted at in Halleck's letter, but when Mr. Stanton visited Sherman at Savannah, the latter understood that his mind was disabused of any unfavorable impressions he may have had. Mr. Stanton had assembled a score of the leading colored preachers as the most intelligent representatives of their race, and examined them by written questions respecting their hopes and desires, their attitude in regard to military service, and in regard to living among the whites or separately. He learned that they generally preferred to try life in a separate community of their own, and that they were strongly opposed to the methods by which State agents were trying to enlist them as substitutes for men drafted in the Northern States. He even went so far as to ask these men whether they found Sherman friendly to the colored people's rights and interests or otherwise! The answer was that they had confidence in the general, and thought their concerns could not be in better hands. Some of them had called upon him on his arrival, and now said that they did not think he could have received Mr. Stanton with more courtesy than he showed to them.[10] Sherman's order relating to the allotment of sea-island lands to the freedmen for cultivation, and to the methods of procuring their enlistment as soldiers[11] was drafted while Mr. Stanton was with him, and he affirms that every paragraph had the Secretary's approval.[12]

    In his feelings toward the men chiefly responsible for secession and the war, Sherman had never measured his words when expressing his condemnation and wrath. In a letter to General Robert Anderson, written only a few days before meeting Johnston in negotiation, he had spoken with deepest feeling of his satisfaction that Anderson was to raise again the flag at Fort Sumter on April 14th (the fatal day on which also Lincoln died), saying he was "glad that it falls to the lot of one so pure and noble to represent our country in a drama so solemn, so majestic, and so just." To him it looked like "a retribution decreed by Heaven itself." Reminded by this thought of those who had caused this horrid war, he exclaimed: "But the end is not yet. The brain that first conceived the thought must burst in anguish, the heart that pulsated with hellish joy must cease to beat, the hand that pulled the first laniard must be palsied, before the wicked act begun in Charleston on the 13th of April, 1861, is avenged. But 'mine, not thine, is vengeance,' saith the Lord, and we poor sinners must let him work out the drama to its close."[13] Such was the man who went to meet General Johnston on the 17th of April; and in considering what he then did, we must take into the account the principles, the convictions, and the feelings which were part of his very nature.

Gen. Robert Anderson, USA

    Still further, we must remember that he had, less than three weeks before, a personal conference with the President at City Point, and had obtained from him personally the views he held with regard to the terms he was prepared to grant to the several rebel States as well as to the armies which might surrender, and the method by which he expected to obtain an acknowledgment of

City Point, Virginia (left).

The
City Point
Conference

Grant's City Point headquarters (above).

President Lincoln met with Admiral David D. Porter, General William T. Sherman, and Geneneral Ulysses S. Grant at Grant's headquarers in City Point, Virginia, to make sure everyone was clear about his wishes for a post-war South (right).

submission from some legally constituted authority, without dealing in any way with the Confederate civil government. General Sherman is conclusive authority as to what occurred at a conference which was in the nature of instructions to him from the Commander-in-Chief; and the more carefully we examine contemporaneous records, the stronger becomes the conviction that he has accurately reported what occurred at that meeting.

"Mr. Lincoln was full and frank in his conversation," says Sherman, "assuring me that in his mind he was all ready for the civil reorganization of affairs at the South as soon as the war was over; and he distinctly authorized me to assure Governor Vance and the people of North Carolina that as soon as the rebel armies laid down their arms and resumed their civil pursuits, they would at once be guaranteed all their rights as citizens of a common country; and that to avoid anarchy, the State governments then in existence, with their civil functionaries, would be recognized by him as the government *de facto* till Congress could provide others."[14]

Gen. Godfrey Weitzel, USA

When the general met Mr. Graham and others, he was aware that General Weitzel at Richmond had authorized the Virginia State government to assemble, Mr. Lincoln being on the ground. The views expressed in the famous interview at City Point had taken practical shape. In correspondence with Johnston while they were awaiting action on the first convention, Sherman referred to Weitzel's action as a reason for confidence that there would be "no trouble on the score of recognizing existing State governments."[15]

With the burden of the terrible news of Lincoln's assassination, Sherman went up to Durham Station to meet the Confederate general on the 17th of April. His grief was mingled with gloomy thoughts of the future, for it was natural that he as well as the authorities at Washington should at first think of the great crime as part of a system of desperate men to destroy both the civil and the military leaders of the country, and to disperse the armies into bands of merciless guerillas who would try the effect of anarchy now that civilized military operations had failed. We did injustice to the South in thinking so, but it was inevitable that such should be the first impression. As soon as we mingled a little with the leading soldiers and statesmen of the South we learned better, and the period of such apprehensions was a brief one, though terrible while it lasted.

But we must here consider what were the motives and purposes which, on his part, Johnston represented, when he came from Greensborough to meet his great opponent. To understand these we must trace rapidly the course of events within his military lines. When Petersburg was taken and Richmond evacuated, Mr. Davis with the members of his cabinet went to Danville, where he remained for a few days, protected by a small force under General H. H. Walker.[16] Beauregard was at Greensborough, collecting detachments to resist an expedition which General Stoneman was leading through the mountains from Tennessee.[17] Johnston was at Smithfield with the main body of his forces, watching our army at Goldsborough and preparing to retreat toward Lee as soon as the latter might escape from Grant and give a rendezvous at Danville or Greensborough. The retreat from Petersburg made a union east of Danville probably impracticable.[18]

Grant's persistent and vigorous pursuit soon turned Lee away from the Danville road at Burkesville, pushed him toward Lynchburg, and destroyed all hope of union with Johnston. Davis had no direct communication with Lee after reaching Danville, and his position there being unsafe, after Grant had occupied Burkesville, he went to Greensborough.[19] From Danville, on the 10th, he telegraphed Johnston that he had a report of the surrender of Lee, which there was little room to doubt. He also asked Johnston to meet him at Greensborough to confer as to future action.[20] The dispatch was, by some accident, prevented from reaching Johnston on the 10th, and Davis repeated it on the

Gen. George Stoneman, USA

11th, so that the news reached the Confederate headquarters only a day before we got it, on our march from Smithfield. On the same day (11th) Davis informed Governor Vance of the disaster, and suggested a meeting with him also.[21] He also forwarded to Johnston the suggestion of Beauregard (which he approved), that all the Confederate forces north of Augusta should concentrate at Salisbury.

The best evidence that Vance regarded the cause of the Confederacy as lost is found in his resolve to send a deputation to meet Sherman without waiting to confer with Davis. Johnston issued on the 11th his orders for the continued march of his army westward from Raleigh along the railroad,[22] and himself proceeded to Greensborough by train, to have the appointed conference. Whilst Davis and he were together on the 12th, Stoneman's cavalry, which had been in the vicinity the day before and had made a break in the Danville road, was heard of at Shallow Ford, on the Yadkin, about thirty miles west. Part of the troops at Greensborough were at once sent to Salisbury, which was about the same distance from the Yadkin ford.[23] At the same time came a cipher dispatch from Colonel Anderson of Johnston's staff, whom the latter had left at Raleigh, saying that Governor Vance was sending Messrs. Graham and Swain to meet Sherman, presumably by permission of Hardee, who was senior officer in Johnston's absence. Colonel Anderson had taken the responsibility of asking Hampton not to let them pass his cavalry outposts.[24] By Davis's direction, Johnston at once telegraphed Hardee to arrest the delegation and to permit no intercourse with us except under proper military flag of truce.[25] Vance was of course informed by Hardee, and replied that he intended nothing subversive of Davis's prerogative or without consulting him. He also said that Johnston was aware of his purpose.[26] In saying further, however, that the initiative had been on Sherman's part, he was dissembling.[27] The difficulty put in the way of his representatives in getting beyond the Confederate lines is thus accounted for, as well as his failure to remain in Raleigh on our arrival. Davis found it politic to accept the explanation,[28] but we may safely assume that the matter was discussed between him and Johnston, and that it led to its discussion with his cabinet also; for Johnston remained with him till the 14th, leaving to Hardee the direction of the army on the march, which was ordered to be pressed towards Greensborough.[29] The troops at Danville were called to the same rendezvous, and General Echols, with those in West Virginia, was ordered to make his way through the mountains to the northwestern part of South Carolina.[30]

Judah P. Benjamin

In a formal conference with his advisers on the 13th (Thursday), all of the cabinet officers except Benjamin declared themselves of Johnston's and Beauregard's opinion, that a further prosecution of the war was hopeless; that the Southern Confederacy was in fact overthrown, and that the wise thing to do was to make at once the best terms possible.[31] Davis argued that the crisis might rouse the Southern people to new and desperate efforts, and that overtures for peace on the basis of submission were premature. The general opinion, however, was so strong against him that he reluctantly yielded, and, to make sure that he should not be committed further than he meant, he himself dictated, and Mr. Mallory, the Secretary of the Navy, wrote, the letter to Sherman, signed by Johnston, asking for an armistice between all the armies, if General Grant would consent, "the object being to permit the civil authorities to enter into the needful arrangements to terminate the existing war."[32] The form of each sentence of the letter is significant, in view of its authorship, but most so is the plain meaning of that just quoted, to make a complete surrender upon such terms as the National government should dictate. In like manner the opening sentence, "The results of the recent campaign in Virginia have changed the relative military condition of the belligerents," was a confession in diplomatic form of final defeat. Before sending the letter to Sherman, Johnston copied it with his own hand, in order, no doubt, to have a duplicate for his own protection, as well as to preserve secrecy.[33]

Sherman lost not a moment in answering, 1st, that he had power and was willing to arrange a suspension of hostilities between the armies under their respective commands, indicating a halt on both sides on the 15th; 2d, that he offered as a basis the terms given Lee at Appomattox: 3d,

Stephen R. Mallory

interpreting Johnston's reference to "other armies" which he desired the truce to include as referring to Stoneman (whom we had heard of in Raleigh as burning railway bridges on both sides of Greensborough[34]), he said that Stoneman was under his command, and that he would obtain from Grant a suspension of other movements from Virginia.[35] All this was strictly within the limits of Sherman's military authority and discretion.

The 15th of April (Saturday) was a day of pouring rain, making the roads almost impassable for wagons, as they were already cut up by the retreating army and by our advance. Sherman expected a reply from Johnston early, for he had directed Kilpatrick on Friday afternoon to send his answer at once to the Confederate lines.[36] He was annoyed at the delay, and sent up Major

McCoy of his staff to Morrisville on the railway, where Kilpatrick's headquarters were, taking with him a telegraph operator to open an office there. But Kilpatrick had gone to his own outposts toward Hillsborough, and his staff seem to have been in no hurry to forward Sherman's letter, so that it was delivered to Hampton at sundown of the 15th instead of the 14th.[37] A locomotive engine was sent to McCoy on Sunday (16th), and with it he went on to Durham, taking his telegrapher along. Some torpedoes had been found on the road below, and McCoy diminished the risk from any others, by putting some empty cars ahead of the locomotive to explode them if there should be any. He got through safely, however, found Kilpatrick at Durham, opened telegraphic communication with headquarters at Raleigh, was authorized to read and transmit by the wire Johnston's reply, and so was able before night to give his impatiently waiting chief the Confederate general's proposal to meet in conference between the lines next morning, and to return Sherman's consent.[38]

Meanwhile Kilpatrick had been sending dispatches saying he did not believe Johnston could be trusted, that his whole army was marching on, that the delay was a ruse to gain time, and that no confidence could be placed "in the word of a rebel, no matter what may be his position. He is but a traitor at best."[39] Sherman answered: "I have faith in General Johnston's personal sincerity, and do not believe he would use a subterfuge to cover his movements. He could not stop the movement of his troops till he got my letter, which I hear was delayed all day yesterday by your adjutants' not sending it forward." His faith in Johnston's honorable dealing was justified, but the delay had brought the Confederate infantry to the neighborhood of Greensborough.[40]

On the 15th Sherman had sent both to Grant and to the Secretary of War copies of Johnston's overture and his own answer. He added that he should "be careful not to complicate any points of civil policy;" that he had invited Governor Vance to return to Raleigh with the civil officers of the State, and that ex-Governor Graham, Messrs. Badger, Moore, Holden, and others all agreed "that the war is over and that the States of the South must resume their allegiance, subject to the Constitution and laws of Congress, and that the military power of the South must submit to the National arms. This great fact once admitted," he said, "all the details are easy of arrangement."[41] He directed this to be sent by a swift steamer to Fort Monroe and from there by telegraph to Washington. As this dispatch was sent part of the way by telegraph, it should have reached Washington more than three days ahead of the convention signed on the 18th and carried to the capital by Major Hitchcock, who left Raleigh in the night of that day:[42] but no answer seems to have been made to it, unless it be in a dispatch of Grant on the 20th in which he directed the movement of Howard's and Slocum's armies to City Point in case Johnston surrendered.[43]

Sherman made his Confederate counterpart aware of Lincoln's death at Bennett Place.

On Monday (April 17th), with the burden of the knowledge of Lincoln's assassination on his mind, Sherman went up to Durham by rail, accompanied by a few officers. There he met General Kilpatrick, who furnished a cavalry company as an escort, and led-horses to mount the party.[44] The bearer of the flag of truce and a trumpeter were in advance, followed by part of the escort, the general and his officers came next, the little cavalcade closing with the rest of the escort in due order. They rode about five miles on the Hillsborough road, when they met General Wade Hampton advancing with a flag from the other side. The house of a Mr. Bennett, near by, was made the place of conference. When Sherman and Johnston were alone, the dispatch announcing Mr. Lincoln's murder was shown the Confederate, and as he read it, Sherman tells us, beads of perspiration stood out on his forehead, his face showed the horror and distress he felt, and he denounced the act as a disgrace to the age.[45] Both realized the danger that terrible results would follow if hostilities should be resumed, and both were impelled to yield whatever seemed possible to bring the war to an immediate end. In this praiseworthy spirit their discussion was carried on, Johnston saying that "the greatest possible calamity to the South had happened."[46]

Johnston's first point was that his proposal of the 14th had been that the civil authorities should negotiate as to the terms of peace, while the armistice should continue. Sherman could not deal with the Confederate civil government or recognize it. It could only dissolve and vanish when the separate states should make their submission, and these were the only governments *de facto* with whom dealings could be had. Postponing this matter, they proceeded to the practical one,—the terms that could be assured to the armies of the South and to the States.

Here they found themselves not far apart. As to the troops, nothing more liberal could be asked than the terms already given to Lee. Sherman knew of Mr. Lincoln's willingness that the State governments should continue to act, if they began by declaring the Confederacy dissolved by defeat, and the authority of the United States recognized and acknowledged. He had no knowledge of any change in the policy of the government in this respect, and what he had said to Governor Vance's delegation was satisfactory to both negotiators.

But how as to amnesty? Here Sherman was also able to give Lincoln's own words, declaring his desire that the people in general should be assured of all their rights of life, liberty, and property, and the political rights of citizens of a common country on their complete submission. Lincoln wanted no more lives sacrificed, and would use his power to make amnesty complete. He could not control the legislative or the judicial department of the government, but he spoke for himself as executive. An agreement was easy here also.

What, then, as to slavery? Sherman regarded it utterly dead in the regions occupied by the Confederates at the time of the Emancipation Proclamation (Jan. 1, 1863), and Johnston frankly admitted that surrender in view of the whole situation acknowledged the end of the system which had been the great stake in the war.[47] The Thirteenth Amendment of the Constitution, abolishing slavery, had then been accepted by twenty States, Arkansas did so three days later, and the six Northern States which had been delayed in action upon it were as certain to ratify as that a little time should roll round.[48] It was therefore no figure of speech to say that slavery was dead: Sherman, Johnston, and Breckinridge knew it to be true. But Johnston urged that to secure the prompt and peaceful acquiescence of the whole South, it was undesirable to force upon them irritating acknowledgments even of what they tacitly admitted to themselves was true; further, that the subject was not included in the scope of a military convention. If slavery was in fact abolished by Mr. Lincoln's proclamation, it was for Congress and the courts so to declare it, and two soldiers arranging the surrender had no call to assert all the legal consequences which would flow from the act. Sherman yielded to this argument, not from any doubt as to the fact of freedom, but from a certainty of it so complete that he would not prolong dispute to obtain a formal assent to it. He was the more ready to do so as he insisted that he acted simply as the representative of the Executive as Commander-in-Chief, and neither could nor would promise immunity from prosecutions under indictments or confiscation-laws. He said also that whilst he agreed with Mr. Lincoln in hoping no executions or long imprisonments would occur, he advised the leading men in the Confederate Government to get out of the country.

As to the disposal of the arms in the hands of the Confederate soldiers from North Carolina to Texas, both knew that little of practical moment depended on the form of the agreement. So many arms were thrown away, so many were concealed by soldiers who loved the weapons they had carried, that even in our own ranks no satisfactory collection of them could be made. But a real and present apprehension with both officers was the scattering of armed men in guerilla bands. If the law-abiding were disarmed and those who scattered and refused to give up their weapons were at large, how could the States preserve the peace? To this point Sherman said he attached most importance. This was not an afterthought when defending his action; he wrote it to Grant in the letter transmitting the terms when they were made.[49] The same thought was forced

home on the Confederates by their experience at the time. Before the negotiations were finally concluded, bands of paroled men from Lee's army, and stragglers were able to stop trains on the railroad on which Johnston's army was dependent for supplies, and it would have been intolerable to leave the country at the mercy of that class.[50] To keep the troops of each State under discipline till they deposited the arms at State capitals, where United States garrisons would be, and where the final disposal of them would be "subject to the future action of Congress," seemed prudent and safe; and this was agreed to.[51]

Gen. John C. Breckinridge, CSA

In the first day's conference it seemed clear that the generals could easily agree upon all they thought essential, except the exclusion of Mr. Davis and his chief civil officers from any part in the negotiations and making the terms of amnesty general. An adjournment to Tuesday was had to give Johnston time to consult with General Breckinridge, the Secretary of War, and for Sherman to reflect further on the amnesty question.[52] As soon as the latter reached Raleigh, he dispatched to Grant, through a staff officer at New Berne, a brief report of the "full and frank interchange of opinions" with Johnston. "He evidently seeks to make terms for Jeff. Davis and his cabinet," he said. The adjournment was mentioned with its reason; and to negative any thought that he might neglect military advantages by the delay, he said, "We lose nothing in

time, as by agreement both armies stand still, and the roads are drying up, so that
if I am forced to pursue, we will be able to make better speed. There is great
danger that the Confederate armies will dissolve and fill the whole land with
robbers and assassins, and I think this is one of the difficulties that Johnston
labors under. The assassination of Mr. Lincoln shows one of the elements in the
rebel army which will be almost as difficult to deal with as the main armies."[53]

When the two generals met again on Tuesday, General Breckinridge was
with Johnston's party, and the latter requested that he might take part in the
conference; but Sherman adhered to his position that he would deal only with the
military officers and objected to Breckinridge as Secretary of War. Johnston
suggested that he might be present simply as a general officer, but adding that
his personal relations to Mr. Davis would greatly aid in securing final approval
of anything to which he assented. With this understanding he was allowed to be
present. Mr. Reagan, Postmaster-General, had also come with Breckinridge to
General Hampton's headquarters, but did not proceed further. He was busy there,
Johnston tells us, in throwing into form the terms which the general thought
were fairly included in the conversational comparison of views on the previous
day, with the exception of the amnesty, which was made general without
exceptions.[54] This must, of course, have been from notes written at Johnston's
dictation.

Sherman was now informed that the Confederate general had authority
to negotiate a military convention for the surrender of all the Confederate
armies, and that if the terms could be agreed upon, the Davis government would
disband, like the armies, and use the influence of its members to secure the
submission of all the several States. Johnston, on his part, would be content with
the conclusions informally reached on Monday, except that he wanted the
principle inserted of amnesty without exceptions. Mr. Reagan's draft was
produced and read.[55] It contained a preamble stating motives for the action
proposed, and professed to be no more than a basis for further negotiation. A
note appended to it referred to several things necessary to a conclusion of the
business which might be subsequently added. The preamble, as well as this note,
was no proper part of the terms, and Sherman entirely objected to any preamble
of the kind, wishing to include only the things necessary to an agreement. He
therefore took his pen, and then and there wrote off rapidly his own expression
of the points he had intended to agree to, but explicitly as a "memorandum or
basis" for submission to their principals.

They were, *First*, the continuance of the armistice, terminable on short
notice; *Second*, the disbanding of all the Confederate armies under parol and
deposit of their arms subject to the control of the National government; *Third*,
recognition by the Executive of existing State governments; *Fourth*, re-
establishment of Federal Courts; *Fifth*, guaranty for the future of general rights

of person, property, and political rights "so far as the Executive can;" *Sixth*, freedom for the people from disturbance on account of the past, by "the Executive authority of the government;" the *seventh* item was a general résumé of results aimed at.[56] The most striking difference between this statement and that which Mr. Reagan had drawn, besides the omission of the preamble, was the express limitation of the proposed action by the powers of the National executive, with neither promise nor suggestion as to what the courts or Congress might or might not do.

In transmitting the memorandum through General Grant, Sherman wrote that the point to which he attached most importance was "that the dispersion and disbandment of those armies is done in such a manner as to prevent their breaking up into guerilla bands," whilst there was no restriction on our right to military occupation.[57] As to slavery, he said, "Both generals Johnston and Breckinridge admitted that slavery was dead, and I could not insist on embracing it in such a paper, because it can be made with the States in detail."[58] He also referred to the financial question, and the necessity of stopping war expenditures and getting the officers and men of the army home to work. Writing to Halleck as chief of staff at the same time, he referred to the same topics, expressed his belief, from all he saw and heard, that "even Mr. Davis was not privy to the diabolical plot" of assassination, but that it was "the emanation of a set of young men of the South who are very devils."[59] He told Halleck that Johnston informed him that Stoneman's cavalry had been at Salisbury, but was then near Statesville, which was on the road back to Tennessee, about forty miles west of Salisbury and double that distance west of Greensborough.

A week now intervened, in which the important papers were journeying to Washington and the orders of the government coming back. On the 20th Sherman had occasion to inform Johnston of steps he had taken to enforce the details of the truce, and as evidence that he had not mistaken Mr. Lincoln's views in regard to the State governments, he enclosed a late paper showing that "in Virginia the State authorities are acknowledged and invited to resume their lawful functions."[60] The convention seemed therefore in harmony with the course actually pursued by the administration at Washington, and the negotiators were justified in feeling reassured.

Another day passed, and as other incidents in the relations of the armies needed to be communicated to Johnston, Sherman recurred again to the encouraging feature of the leave to assemble the Virginia legislature, but added some reflections on points which he thought might require more explicit treatment than they had given, and he suggested Johnston's conference with the best Southern men, so that he might be ready to act without delay if modifications should be required in the final convention. "It may be," he said, "that the lawyers will want us to define more minutely what is meant by the guaranty of rights of person and property. It may be construed into a compact for us to undo the past as to the rights of slaves, and 'leases of plantations' on the Mississippi, of 'vacant and abandoned' plantations. I wish you would talk to the best men you have on these points, and if possible, let us, in the final convention, make these points so clear as to leave no room for angry controversy. I believe if the South would simply and publicly declare what we all feel, that slavery is dead, that you would inaugurate an era of peace and prosperity that would soon efface the ravages of the past four years of war. Negroes would remain in the South and afford you abundance of cheap labor, which otherwise will be driven away, and it will save the country the senseless discussions which have kept us all in hot water for fifty years. Although, strictly speaking, this is no subject of a military convention, yet I am honestly convinced that our simple declaration of a result will be accepted as good law everywhere. Of course I have not a single word from Washington on this or any other point of our agreement, but I know the effect of such a step by us will be universally accepted."[61]

On the same day (21st), he was replying to a letter from an acquaintance of former days residing at Wilmington. In this reply he spoke out more vigorously his own sentiments: "The idea of war to perpetuate slavery in the year 1861 was an insult to the intelligence of the age." War being begun by the South, "it was absurd to suppose we were bound to respect that kind of property or any kind of property. . . . The result is nearly accomplished, and is what you might have foreseen."[62]

On the 23d he sent a bundle of newspapers to Johnston and Hardee, giving the developments of the assassination plot and the hopes that the Sewards would recover. In the unofficial note accompanying them, he said: "The feeling North on this subject is more intense than anything that ever occurred before. General Ord at Richmond has recalled the permission given for the Virginia legislature, and I fear much the assassination of the President will give a bias to the popular mind which, in connection with the desire of our politicians, may thwart our purpose of recognizing 'existing local governments.' But it does seem to me there must be good sense enough left on this continent to give order and shape to the now disjointed elements of government. I believe this assassination of Mr. Lincoln will do the cause of the South more harm than any event of the war, both at home and abroad, and I doubt if the Confederate military authorities had any more complicity with it than I had. I am thus frank with you, and have asserted as much to the War Department. But I dare not say as much for Mr. Davis or some of the civil functionaries, for it seems the plot was fixed for March 4, but delayed awaiting some instructions from Richmond."[63]

The whole tenor of this letter speaks most clearly the faith which personal intercourse with Johnston had given Sherman in his honor and his sincerity of desire that the war should end. The same had been expressed in an official note of the same date in which Sherman had said in regard to his directions to General Wilson in Georgia: "I have almost exceeded the bounds of prudence in checking him without the means of direct communication, and only did so on my absolute faith in your personal character."[64] The faith was not misplaced and was not disappointed.

The correspondence thus quoted reveals to us Sherman's thoughts from day to day, the real opinions and sentiments which he intended to embody in the convention, and his recognition of the probability that its provisions would need more explicit definition before the final acts of negotiation. It shows, too, how frank he was in warning Johnston that the terrible crime at Washington had changed the situation. It seems indisputable that this open-hearted dealing between the generals made it much easier for them to come together on the final terms, by having revealed to Johnston the motives and convictions which animated his opponent in seeking the blessing of peace as well as in applying the scourge of war.

As further evidence of what Sherman told us, his subordinates, of the terms agreed upon, I quote the entry in my diary of what I understood them to be, on the 19th, the day following the signing of the convention, after personal conversation with the general: "Johnston's army is to separate, the troops going to their several States; at the State capitals they are to surrender their arms and all public property. Part of the arms are to be left to the State governments and the rest turned over to the United States. The officers and soldiers are not to be punished by the United States Government for their part in the war, but all are left liable to private prosecutions and indictments in the courts."[65]

In the evening of the 23d Sherman heard of the arrival at Morehead City of Major Hitchcock, his messenger to Washington, and he at once notified Johnston that the dispatches would reach him in the morning. He asked the latter to be ready "to resume negotiations when the contents of the dispatches are known."[66] When Major Hitchcock came up on a night train reaching Raleigh at six in the morning, to Sherman's great surprise General Grant came also, unheralded and unannounced.[67]

Chapter XLIX Notes

1. Sherman Letters, p. 63.
2. Sherman Letters, p. 77.
3. *Id.*, p. 83.
4. *Id.*, p. 106.
5. *Id.*, p. 222.
6. Official Records, vol, xxxii. pt. ii. p. 280.

7. Official Records, vol. xxxii. pt ii. p. 279.
8. *Id.*, vol. xliv. p. 836.
9. Official Records, vol. xlvii. pt. ii. p. 36.
10. *Id.*, p. 41.
11. Official Records, vol. xlvii. pt. ii. p. 60.
12. Memoirs, vol. ii. p. 250.
13. Official Records, vol. xlvii. pt. iii. p. 107.
14. Sherman's Memoirs, vol. ii. p. 327.
15. Official Records, vol. xlvii. pt. iii. p. 266.
16. Official Records, vol. xlvii. pt. iii. pp. 741, 750.
17. *Id.*, p. 751.
18. *Id.*, pp. 682, 737.
19. Official Records, vol. xlvii. pt. iii. pp. 750, 787.
20. *Id.*, p. 777.
21. *Id.*, p. 787.
22. *Id.*, p. 789.
23. *Id.*, p. 791.
24. Official Records, vol. xlvii. pt. iii. p. 791.
25. *Ibid.*
26. *Id.*, p. 792.
27. See the letters, *Id.*, p. 178.
28. *Id.*, p. 792.
29. *Id.*, pp. 796, 797.
30. *Id.*, pp. 795, 796.
31. Johnston's Narrative, pp. 397-400.
32. Official Records, vol. xlvii. pt. iii. p. 206.
33. The only difference is that in his copy he put the date of the 13th at its head (the true date), whilst the original which he says he sent to Sherman (Narr., p. 400) was dated the 14th, when it would be sent from his outposts; a bit of forethought on Mr. Davis's part, which guarded against Sherman's suspicion that it had been prepared at a distance and had travelled more than a day's journey. Both of the duplicates are in the war archives, that written by Mr. Mallory having the indorsement in Sherman's own hand of its receipt on the 14th. (Official Records, vol. xlvii. pt. iii. p. 206, note.) In the Records Sherman's indorsement of the receipt of Johnston's dispatch is "12 night." This seems to be a clerical error, and should be "noon." (See *Id.*, pp. 209, 215, 216, and Sherman's Memoirs, vol. ii. p. 346.) Mr. Davis's account is not inconsistent with Johnston's, which he had seen. (Rise and Fall, vol. ii. pp. 681, 684.)
34. Official Records, vol. xlvii. pt. iii. p. 197.
35. *Id.*, p. 207.
36. *Id.*, p. 215.

37. *Id.*, p. 222, 233, 234.

38. Official Records, vol. xlvii. pt. iii. pp. 229-231.

39. *Id.*, pp. 224, 233.

40. *Id.*, p. 234. Also Johnston's Narrative, p. 401.

41. Official Records, vol. xlvii. pt. iii. p. 221.

42. Official Records, vol. xlvii. pt. iii. p. 246.

43. *Id.*, p. 257.

44. *Id.*, pp. 234, 235.

45. Memoirs, vol. ii. p. 349,

46. Johnston's Narrative, p. 402.

47. Official Records, vol. xlvii. pt. iii. p. 243.

48. Rickey's Constitution, p. 43.

49. Official Records, vol. xlvii. pt. iii. p. 243.

50. *Id.*, pp. 818, 819.

51. *Id.*, pp. 243, 244.

52. Sherman's Memoirs, vol. ii. p. 350; Johnston's Narrative, p. 404.

53. Official Records, vol. xlvii. pt. iii. p. 237.

54. Johnston's Narrative, p. 404.

55. Official Records, vol. xlvii. pt. iii. p. 806.

56. *Id.*, p 243.

57. Official Records, vol. xlvii. pt. iii. p. 243.

58. *Ibid.*

59. *Id.*, p. 245.

60. *Id.*, p. 257.

61. Official Records, vol. xlvii. pt. iii. p. 266.

62. Official Records, vol. xlvii. pt. iii. p. 271.

63. *Id.*, p. 287.

64. *Id.*, p. 286.

65. Official Records, vol. xlvii. pt. i. p. 938.

66. *Id.*, pt. ii. p. 287.

67. *Id.*, p. 286.

CHAPTER L

THE SECOND SHERMAN—JOHNSTON CONVENTION—SURRENDER

Davis's last cabinet meeting—Formal opinions approving the "Basis"—"The Confederacy is conquered"—Grant brings disapproval from the Johnston administration—Sherman gives notice of the termination of the truce—No military disadvantage from it—Sherman's vindication of himself—Grant's admirable conduct—Johnston advises Davis to yield—Capitulation assented to, but a volunteer cavalry force to accompany Davis's flight—A new conference at Durham—Davis's imaginary treasure—Grant's return to Washington—Terms of the parole given by Johnston's army—The capitulation complete—Schofield and his army to carry out the details—The rest of Sherman's army marches north—His farewell to Johnston—Order announcing the end of the war—Johnston's fine reply—Stanton's strange dispatch to the newspapers—Its tissue of errors—Its baseless objections—Sherman's exasperation—Interference with his military authority over his subordinates—Garbling Grant's dispatch—Sherman strikes back—Breach between Sherman and Halleck—It also grew out of the published matter—Analysis of the facts—My opinion as recorded at the time.

When Grant reached Sherman's headquarters on the morning of the 24th of April, Johnston had not yet been notified of the action of the Confederate government as to the agreed "Basis" of surrender. Having got Sherman's dispatch of the evening before, he telegraphed to General Breckinridge, the Secretary of War at Greensborough, that there must be immediate readiness to act.[1] Breckinridge, however, had gone to Charlotte, about eighty miles down the road, near the South Carolina line, where Mr. Davis held the last meeting of his cabinet, and procured from each of them his formal, written opinion and advice. Davis himself now telegraphed the result to Johnston, saying: "Your action is approved. You will so inform General Sherman, and if the like authority be given by the Government of the United States to complete the arrangement, you will proceed on the 'Basis' adopted."[2] He added that further instructions would be given as to the subordinate details which, by common consent, must be added to the "Basis" to perfect it.

The cabinet opinions were unanimous in favor of approving the "Basis." Benjamin's, Reagan's, and Attorney-General Davis's were dated the 22d, Breckinridge's the 23d, and Mallory's the 24th.[3]

In varying words they all admitted what Mallory put most tersely, in saying "The Confederacy is conquered."[4] Several of them discussed the possibility of carrying on a guerilla warfare, but could see in it no useful result. They agreed that if Johnston retreated to the Gulf States, the troops would disperse spontaneously. Virginia and North Carolina would separately withdraw from the Confederacy, and the other States would follow. Benjamin expressed the common opinion that the terms of the convention "exact only what the victor always requires,—the relinquishment by his foe of the object for which the struggle was commenced."[5] He also well formulated their judgment that, as political head, Davis could not make peace by dissolving the Confederacy; but as commander-in-chief he could ratify the military convention disbanding the armies. "He can end hostilities. The States alone can act in dissolving the Confederacy and returning to the Union according to the terms of the convention."[6] Reagan alone spoke of hopes that by submission the States might procure advantages not mentioned in the "Basis," and found comfort in the fact that it contained "no direct reference to the question of slavery."[7] Taken together, these important documents contain the strongest possible admission of the utter ruin of the Confederacy and of the simple truth that there was nothing left for them but to surrender at discretion, with such dignity as they might. Of themselves the cabinet opinions changed the situation, and made it impossible to resume plans of further resistance after the convention was rejected at Washington. With them the Confederate Government vanished.

For it was a disapproval that Grant had brought. On receiving the "Memorandum, or Basis," from Sherman, on the 21st, he had at once seen that the latter had acted in ignorance of the facts: first, that Mr. Lincoln had himself, two days before his death, withdrawn the permission for the Virginia legislature to assemble; and second, that he had, a month before Lee's surrender, directed that military negotiations should not treat of any subject of civil policy. In view, therefore, of the tendency to severity which followed the assassination, it was evident that the convention would not be approved, and, as soon as action had been taken by the President in cabinet meeting, Grant wrote a calm and friendly letter to Sherman, in explanation of the rejection of the "Basis," inclosing

Stanton's formal notice and order to resume hostilities.[8] These were intrusted to Major Hitchcock, but, as we have seen, Grant accompanied the messenger in person.

Sherman having, only the day before, learned of the change of policy with regard to Virginia, and notified Johnston of its probable effect, was prepared in part for the disapproval, and was personally glad to be rid of political negotiation. He made no objection or remonstrance, but even before discussing the subject with Grant, wrote his notice to Johnston of the termination of the truce within forty-eight hours, as agreed. With this he sent a note stating his orders "not to attempt civil negotiations," and demanding surrender of Johnston's own army "on the same terms as were given General Lee at Appomattox."[9] These dispatches were dated at six in the morning of the 24th, a few minutes after Grant's arrival.[10]

Sherman then explained to the General-in-Chief the military situation, the position of his several corps, his readiness to make the race with Johnston for Charlotte, the completed repair of the railroad through Raleigh to Durham, the accumulation of supplies, and the improved condition of the country roads. The truce had worked him no disadvantage from a military standpoint, but the contrary. The only thing which annoyed him in the dispatches from Washington was the last sentence in Mr. Stanton's communication to Grant, saying, "The President desires that you proceed immediately to the headquarters of General Sherman and direct operations against the enemy."[11] The implication in this was a distrust of him which was wholly unjust, and he replied to it, "I had flattered myself that by four years' patient, unremitting, and successful labor I deserved no such reminder."[12] In a letter to Grant of the same date he put upon record the fact that he had reason to suppose that his "Memorandum" accurately reflected Mr. Lincoln's ideas and purposes, and that he was wholly uninformed of the instructions in regard to negotiating upon civil questions. He stood by his opinions on the propriety of using the *de facto* governments in the separate States as agents of submission for their people. He pointed out that the military convention did not meddle with the right of the courts to punish past crimes, and stated that he admitted the need of clearer definition as to the guaranty of rights of person and property.[13] The points he thus discussed were those he got from Grant orally, for he had, as yet, no other knowledge of the criticisms made by President Johnson or his cabinet.

Grant's sincere friendship and his freedom from the least desire to exhibit his own power had made him act as a visitor rather than a commander. He appreciated Sherman's perfect readiness to accept the methods dictated by the civil authorities, and saw that his zeal was as ardent as it was at Atlanta or Savannah. The results of the honest frankness of the dealings between Sherman and Johnston were speedily seen. The Confederate general perfectly understood the meaning of the notice to end the truce, and that his great opponent would do his military duty to the uttermost. Whilst ordering his army to be ready to move at the expiration of the truce, he also declared to Mr. Davis, in asking for instructions, that it were better to yield than to have Sherman's army again traverse the country.[14] Davis suggested, through Breckinridge, that the infantry and artillery might be disbanded, but the cavalry and horse-batteries brought off to accompany the high civil officers who would try to reach the Southwest.[15] Johnston replied that this would only provide for saving these functionaries from captivity. This might be done by Mr. Davis moving with a smaller cavalry escort, without losing a moment. To save the people, the country, and the army, an honorable military capitulation ought to be made before the expiration of the armistice. He said that his subordinate commanders did not believe their troops would fight again, and that news was received of the fall of Mobile, with 3,000 prisoners, and the capture of Macon, with a number of prominent generals.[16] Early on the 25th Breckinridge assented to the capitulation, but directed that General Wade Hampton, with the mounted men who chose to follow him, might join the President.[17] Upon this, Johnston wrote Sherman, asking that instead of a surrender and disbanding in the field, his army might have the arrangement for going home in organizations which had been made by the Memorandum of the 18th, giving as a reason that Lee's paroled men were already afflicting the country, collecting in bands which had no means of subsistence but robbery.[18] Sherman then appointed a new conference at Durham, for the 26th, at noon.[19] He had learned from Grant that it was believed at Washington that Davis had with him a large treasure in specie, making for Cuba by way of Florida, and sent at once a dispatch to Admiral Dahlgren, naval commander at Charleston, asking that officer to try to intercept him.[20]

General Grant's complete satisfaction with Sherman's personal attitude and readiness to accept the action of the President was shown in his wish to return at once to Washington. He prepared to start from Raleigh on the morning of the 26th, taking a steamer from New Berne on arriving there.[21] He expected, of course that the surrender would be completed and the result telegraphed him by the time his vessel was ready to start, but he was also moved by delicacy toward Sherman and the desire to relieve him from every appearance of supervision which his stay at Raleigh might give. Sherman, however, was also chivalrous, and requested Grant not to leave till he should see the capitulation finally signed.[22] All this, it must be remembered, was in entire ignorance of the follies perpetrated at the War Department during those days.

The hour fixed for the new conference at Durham was the same at which the armistice would expire; but Sherman, having the troops in readiness to start at a moment's notice, ordered that no movement should be made till his return.[23] An accident to his railroad delayed Johnston two or three hours, but on his arrival a brief conference satisfied him that the only course to pursue was to surrender on the terms given to Lee, and to trust to Sherman's assurance that such arrangements would be made in executing the capitulation as would guard against the evils of the dispersion of his army without means of subsistence, which both officers justly feared. As in Lee's case the language used avoided terms which implied being prisoners of war even momentarily, but provided that after delivering the arms to an ordnance officer at Greensborough (excepting side-arms of officers) and giving an "individual obligation not to take up arms against the Government of the United States, . . . all the officers and men will be permitted to return to their homes, not to be disturbed by the United States authorities so long as they observe their obligation and the laws in force where they may reside."[24]

At half-past seven in the evening Grant was able to write his dispatch to Stanton, Secretary of War, that the surrender was complete, and by using the telegraph to New Berne and Morehead City, and from Fort Monroe to Washington, the news reached Washington at ten in the morning of the 28th.[25] The same evening, and by same means of transmittal, he also informed Halleck at Richmond of the surrender, and recalled all his troops out of Sherman's theatre of operations.[26] After hearing the details of Sherman's conversations with Johnston, and approving the suggestions of liberal arrangements looking to getting the Confederate troops quickly and quietly back to peaceful industry at their homes, Grant parted with us at Raleigh on the 27th, and returned as rapidly as possible to Washington, where the influence of his calm judgment and executive ability was sorely needed.

The orders for National forces in North Carolina except Schofield's troops to march homeward were issued on the 27th. Kilpatrick's division of cavalry was attached to Schofield's command, and the Army of the Ohio thus reinforced was left to garrison the Department of North Carolina.[27] To General Schofield was also intrusted the preparation of the printed paroles for all the troops included in the capitulation, so that there might be uniformity. To him also was committed the conclusion of the supplementary terms needed for the liberal execution of the convention, as had been discussed at the personal meeting of the commanders, at which he had been present.[28] Johnston sent in a draft of what he had understood to be thus informally arranged, the most important items of which were the "loan" to the Confederates of their army animals and wagons for farming purposes, the retention of a portion of their arms to enforce order and discipline till the separate organizations should reach their homes, and the extension of the privileges of the convention to naval officers of the Confederacy.[29] With slight modifications these were accepted by General Schofield and carried out.[30] A large issue of rations to Johnston's troops had been voluntarily added without any request or stipulation.[31] Both parties understood that Johnston's command included all Confederate troops east of the Chattahoochee, though this is not stated in the terms.[32] At the earnest request of the Confederate general, none of our troops were sent up to Greensborough, where his headquarters and principal camp were, until the printing of the paroles was completed and staff officers sent to issue them on April 30th.[33]

Sherman wrote a farewell letter to Johnston on the 27th, telling of his instructions to General Schofield to give him ten days' rations for 25,000 men, "to facilitate what you and I and all good men desire, the return to their homes of the officers and men composing your army."[34] He spoke also of his directions to "loan" to them enough animals fit for farming purposes to insure a crop. Concluding, he said: "Now that war is over, I am as willing to risk my person and reputation as heretofore, to heal the wounds made by the past war, and I think my feeling is shared by the whole army. I also think a similar feeling actuates the mass of your army, but there are some unthinking young men who have no sense or experience, that unless controlled may embroil their neighbors. If we are forced to deal with them, it must be with severity, but I hope they will be managed by the people of the South."[35] His Field Order No. 65, announcing the end of war east of the Chattahoochee, referred to the same purpose "to relieve present wants and to encourage the inhabitants to renew their peaceful pursuits and to restore the relations of friendship among our fellow-citizens and countrymen." He directed that "great care must be taken that all the terms and stipulations on our part be fulfilled with the most scrupulous fidelity, whilst those imposed on our hitherto enemies be received in a spirit becoming a brave and generous army."[36]

A copy of this order was enclosed in Sherman's letter to Johnston, and the latter replied in a similar noble tone. "The enlarged patriotism manifested in these papers," he said, "reconciles me to what I had previously regarded as the misfortune of my life—that of having had you to encounter in the field. The enlightened and humane policy you have adopted will certainly be successful. It is fortunate for the people of North Carolina that your views are to be carried out by one so capable of appreciating them. I hope you are as well represented in the other departments of your command; if so, an early and complete pacification in it may be expected.... The disposition you express to heal the wounds made by the past war has been evident to me in all our interviews. You are right in supposing that similar feelings are entertained by the mass of this army. I am sure that all the leading men in it will exert their influence for that object."[37]

Down to this moment the progress of events had been full of satisfaction to Sherman, and of gratification to his noble ambition. If the implication contained in the order sending Grant in person to his headquarters had pained him, Grant's perfect handling of the situation had prevented the wound being deep, and Sherman was pleased, on the whole, to be relieved of negotiations on all civil questions. But the day after Grant had left him,—when he had issued his admirable Order No. 65, and exchanged chivalrous sentiments with Johnston,—when he had completed his work in his great campaign and, leaving to Schofield the finishing of the administrative task in North Carolina, was turning his face homeward full of anticipation of rejoining family and friends, with his great career in a retrospect which was altogether gratifying—at this culmination of his glory as a soldier and his pride as a patriot, he received the sorest blow and the deepest wound he ever knew.

The mail, on the 28th, brought a copy of the "New York Times," containing Mr. Stanton's now famous dispatch to General Dix dated the 22d, sent for the purpose of general publication, in which he made known the fact that Sherman had entered into a convention with Johnston, that it was disapproved by the President, and that Sherman was ordered to resume hostilities.[38] Had the newspaper publication stopped here, it would still have been a grave indiscretion, for the news of what was done in Washington usually reached the enemy more promptly than it came to our officers at the front, and the enterprising spies at the capital would have thought their fortunes made by getting on the 22d orders which did not reach Sherman, in fact, till the 24th, with official comments of which the general was ignorant till the 28th.

But this was the least of the faults of this curious document. It said that Sherman had entered into "what is called a basis of peace." No such name was given the paper, and the manner of attributing it misled the public as to its character. It suppressed the fact that the "Memorandum" was by its terms wholly without binding effect if not approved by the President. Without saying so, it persuasively led the reader to believe that Sherman had violated instructions issued by Mr. Lincoln on March 3d, which in fact were never published till it was done in this dispatch, and were wholly unknown to the general, who believed he was acting in accordance with President Lincoln's wishes given him orally at the end of March. It spoke of orders sent by Sherman to Stoneman "to withdraw from Salisbury and join him" as opening "the way for Davis to escape to Mexico or Europe with his plunder, which is reported to be very large." Only complete ignorance of the actual military situation could account for so erroneous a statement. Davis was in the midst of Johnston's whole army, most of which was halted by the truce at Greensborough. Stoneman, on a brilliant cavalry raid, passed rapidly from the North near Greensborough a week before, had struck Salisbury on the 13th, and immediately marched northwest, on his return to East Tennessee, whence he had started. He was at Statesville, forty miles on his way, when Sherman and Johnston made the armistice on the 18th, of which he did not hear a word till he was over the mountains on the 23d.[39]

Sherman first heard of Davis's "plunder" from Grant on the 24th, and immediately asked the navy to frustrate any efforts to take it out of the country.[40]

Davis did not leave the protection of Johnston's army till he knew that Stoneman was far away and his road was clear. In fact, it was only when, after the rejection of the first convention, Johnston had begun negotiations for the separate surrender of his own forces, and further delay would have made him a prisoner. As to the "plunder of the banks" thus published by the Secretary, it turned out that officers of Carolina banks who had taken their assets to Richmond for protection against the perils of war, had taken advantage of the protection of Mr. Davis's escort to carry them home when Richmond fell. As to the specie treasure, rumored to be many millions, about forty thousand dollars was at Greensborough paid to Johnston's soldiers at the rate of $1.17 to each, and the remainder, except a small sum, seems to have been distributed to the cavalry escort, about 3000 strong, which protected Mr. Davis to the Savannah River and then dispersed; the sum was thirty-five dollars per man, given as part of their arrears of pay.[41] The statement in Mr. Stanton's dispatch regarding this "plunder," copied from one received from Halleck, which in turn was based on anonymous rumor, was so couched as to give credit to the imputation that Sherman was to be duped or bribed to allow Davis with his effects, "including this gold plunder," to escape. Not only did the form of the publication give this impression, but that it was in fact so understood and treated is simple matter of history.

Even this was not all. There were appended to this nine enumerated criticisms, most of which were baseless. The first declared that both Sherman and Johnston knew the former had no power to do what was done in the Memorandum. What was done in fact was to transmit to the government, for its acceptance or rejection, Johnston's offer to disband all the remaining armies of the Confederacy, wherever situated, on the terms which were stated. The "Memorandum" itself said that the generals lacked power "to fulfil these terms;" but that they had power to make a truce till the government of the United States considered the proposal, is too plain for serious dispute. Yet Mr. Stanton's criticism implied that the arrangement had not been merely proposed, but had been actually concluded, for the strictures otherwise had no meaning.

The second said that "it was a practical acknowledgment of the rebel government." On the other hand, Sherman had utterly refused to deal with or acknowledge that government in any way. The effect of ratification of the terms would have been its silent disappearance without being named. If the argument were worth anything, it would have been much more potent against the exchanges of prisoners which had been carried on through commissioners of both governments. But the next clause had the added bugbear that the arms when deposited at the State capitals might be "used to conquer and subdue the loyal States." This suppressed the fact that by the "Memorandum" the arms were "to be reported to the chief of ordnance at Washington City subject to the future action of the Congress of the United States." The allowance of arms to local authorities to preserve order was a necessity so self-evident that, in the face of this objection by Mr. Stanton, General Schofield, in supplementary terms of the final surrender, allowed Johnston's troops to retain part of the arms in this way, and no whisper of further objection was made.[42]

The third objection was that "it undertook to re-establish the rebel State governments that had been overthrown." This was untrue in fact. It proposed that the executive should recognize actually existing governments *de facto* in the States, for the purpose of renouncing the Confederacy and acknowledging under oath their allegiance to the United States. For the purpose of such submission, it would seem clear that it would be an advantage to have it made by Vance, and Magrath, and Brown, and the rest who had been the real rebels, rather than by new men whose essential representative character might be denied. The subsequent history of reconstruction gives small support to the opinion that anything was gained which might not have been got more effectively by dictating the civil changes and terms of peace to these old State governments rather than to such provisional makeshifts as were afterward used. But the objection was, after all, not against Sherman, but against the dead Lincoln under whose oral authority Sherman was acting, and who had put the same in clearest written terms in his correspondence with General Weitzel and Judge Campbell after Richmond was in our possession.[43]

The fourth criticism was that by the terms proposed the State governments "would be enabled to re-establish slavery." Apart from the admissions of leading men of the South, and the facts already collated,[44] Mr. Stanton, in saying this, ignored the Proclamation of Emancipation, on which, in his conversation with Judge Campbell, Mr. Lincoln had been entirely willing to rest. The Southern jurist had recognized the solidity of the legal ground "that if the proclamation of the President be valid as law, it has already operated and vested rights." This the judge had stated to his fellow-citizens as a fact in the situation not to be ignored, and had repeated it in his letter of April 7th to General Weitzel in a stronger form, if possible, saying, "The acceptance of the Union involves acceptance of his proclamation, if it be valid in law."[45] The condition of its legal validity was not an insertion by Campbell—it was the expression of Mr. Lincoln himself, conceding the authority of the courts to pass upon the question as he had done in his amnesty proclamation.[46] Mr. Stanton had these things before him, hardly a fortnight old, when he made his singular publication. They add no little to the difficulty of determining the true motives of his appeal to the public.

The fifth objection was the possibility of resulting liability for the rebel debts, which could hardly have been seriously meant.

The sixth was that it put in dispute the loyal State governments and the new State of West Virginia. As to the latter, the "Memorandum" was based on Mr. Lincoln's action in Virginia, and assumed that question to have been determined, so far as the executive was concerned. The criticism, like some of the rest, was aimed at what Mr. Lincoln had done, which was thus flogged over Sherman's shoulders; for the latter was, as we have to reiterate, ignorant that on Mr. Lincoln's return to Washington he had been induced to cancel what he had done. From any point of view but that of a momentary party advantage, it is hard to see the evil of submitting contesting State governments to the decision of the Supreme Court. Those of Louisiana and Arkansas were swept away very soon by Congressional action, and they were the only ones intended to be reached by the Sherman-Johnston "Memorandum."

The seventh declared that it "practically abolished the confiscation laws and relieved the rebels of every degree, who had slaughtered our people, from all pains and penalties for their crimes." Those who had "slaughtered" were primarily the officers and soldiers of the armies, and no fault was found with Grant's extension of amnesty to them by the Appomattox terms. It was true, besides, that the whole male population of the South, of military age, was part of the army, and that even State officers were "furloughed" to enable them to perform public duties of a civil nature. We have seen that Sherman carefully limited immunity to the action of the executive, that he meddled with no laws, and said that all the people were still liable to what the judicial department of the government might do. But he had also acknowledged, upon reflection, that clearer definition would be desirable in this respect, and had asked Johnston to be ready to act upon this.[47] It is our privilege, moreover, judging after the fact, to note how little Stanton's objection practically meant, and how much better Sherman represented the deeper purpose of the American people, since neither Mr. Davis nor any of his chief counsellors suffered "the pains and penalties for their crimes."

The eighth criticism was that the "Memorandum" offered terms "that had been deliberately, repeatedly, and solemnly rejected by President Lincoln, and better terms than the rebels had ever asked in their most prosperous condition." Mr. Stanton could hardly have forgotten, when writing this, that they were in fact not only based on what Sherman had learned of his policy from Mr. Lincoln himself, as we have seen, but they were what President Lincoln had repeatedly offered and the Confederates had repeatedly rejected, the last rejection being after the Hampton Roads conference in the first days of February.[48]

Exactly what was meant by the ninth criticism it is hard to say. It is said that the "Memorandum," if adopted, would "relieve the rebels from the pressure of our victories" and leave them "in condition to renew their efforts to overthrow the United States government and subdue the loyal States whenever their strength was recruited and any opportunity was offered." As it provided for the disarming and disbanding of every Confederate company, left our victorious troops free to garrison every State, and gave protection to individuals only so long as they were obedient to the National government, we must regard the apprehension of new efforts to subdue the loyal States as fantastic and not serious.

It was inevitable that such a manifesto to the public should be greatly exasperating to Sherman. Seeing also the manner in which it was interpreted by the newspapers, he believed that it was purposely so worded as to imply what it did not explicitly assert, and to hold him up to the nation as one little better than a traitor. He was very emphatic in saying that being overruled did not trouble him; it was the public perversion of what he had done, attributing to his "Memorandum" what the publication of its text would have contradicted, which outraged his feelings.[49] Grant frankly adhered to his opinion that in the actual condition of affairs he could not himself advise the ratification of the terms proposed; yet he saw the injustice done Sherman, and condemned it.[50] Their relations continued as cordial as ever, and his influence was potent in preventing further ill results from following the quarrel.

The publication was followed by other acts of Mr. Stanton which increased the irritation. On the 27th of April he informed Halleck, Canby, and Thomas that "Sherman's proceedings" were disapproved, and ordered them to direct their subordinates "to pay no attention to any orders but your own or from General Grant."[51] This was a day after Johnston had made his final surrender under the second convention, and when Grant had been two days with Sherman. It led to Halleck's ordering Meade to pay no attention to the truce, even after the surrender of Johnston was signed, and might have caused serious results if Grant had not been very prompt in giving counter-orders to Halleck.[52] All the department commanders naturally understood Stanton's language in sending Grant to North Carolina, as superseding Sherman in command, though in fact this was not done. They concluded that if any new terms were made with Johnston the action would be in Grant's name, and his signature would verify the truce. But as Grant did not do this, and everything remained in Sherman's hands as before, the actual surrender was ignored and credit refused, by order of the Secretary of War, to the armistice declared while the paroles were being issued. Stanton took no steps to correct this, and for two weeks the strange muddle continued in the Southwest. This came to such a pass that on May 8th Sherman inquired of Grant whether "the Secretary of War's newspaper order" had taken Georgia out of his command.[53] Grant replied, "I know of no order which changes your command in any particular," and, in his patient rôle of peacemaker, suggested that the necessity of prompt communication when Sherman was not in telegraphic communication with Washington had caused some irregularities.[54]

One of the minor incidents in Stanton's course of action throws so strong light on his methods and was so irritating an example of the *suppressio veri* that it must be mentioned. Immediately after his interview with Sherman in the early morning of the 24th, Grant had sent a dispatch to Stanton, which the latter sent to General Dix for publication in the following form: "A dispatch has just been received by this department from General Grant, dated Raleigh, 9 A. M., April 24th. He says: 'I reached here this morning, and delivered to General Sherman the reply to his negotiations with Johnston. Word was immediately sent to Johnston, terminating the truce, and information that civil matters could not be entertained in any convention between army commanders.'"[55] Taken in connection with the previous publication, this was naturally interpreted to mean that Grant had sent the "word" to Johnston, and it strengthened the current against Sherman. The dispatch as sent by Grant was this: "I reached here this morning and delivered to General Sherman the reply to his negotiations with Johnston. *He was not surprised, but rather expected their rejection.* Word was immediately sent to Johnston terminating the truce, and information that civil matters could not be entertained in any convention between army commanders. *General Sherman has been guided in his negotiations with Johnston entirely by what he thought was precedent authorized by the President. He had before him the terms given by me to Lee's army and the call of the rebel legislature of Virginia authorized by General Weitzel, as he supposed with the sanction of the President and myself. At the time of the agreement General Sherman did not know of the withdrawal of authority for the meeting of that legislature. The moment he learned through the papers that authority for the meeting had been withdrawn, he communicated the fact to Johnston as having bearing on the negotiations had.*"[56] I have italicized the omitted parts to show how absolutely essential they were to a true statement of Sherman's attitude, and how grave was the offence against fair dealing to suppress them after the appeal to the public had been made by the first publication. The dispatch is also historically important as proof of the ideal character of Grant's disinterestedness and frank friendship for Sherman in this juncture.

Mr. Stanton's habit of impetuous action without reflection, upon first impressions and imperfect knowledge, was notorious, as was his constitutional inability to admit that he had been in the wrong. Once aroused, he was a fierce combatant, using any weapon that came to hand, inquiring only whether it would hurt his opponent. When obliged to see that he had judged wrongly, his silence was the only confession: he was seldom equal to a candid apology. If a tacit retreat was accepted by the other party, he might endeavor to compensate for the wrong in some other manner.[57]

Sherman was not the man to submit to what he considered and called an outrage, and when made aware of it, he struck back with all his force. He exposed and denounced the perversions of fact and misstatements of what he had done, and demanded the publication of the original "Memorandum" with his statement of its relations to Mr. Lincoln's policy and wishes as stated by the dead President himself. Grant advised him to omit some of the expressions of his official report, but he refused and courted an official investigation, whilst he clearly stated his duty and his purpose to obey without question such orders as were given by competent authority. He was quite too large a man to be made the victim of a manifest wrong, and when once the case was fairly presented, the purity of his motives and the reasonableness of his belief that he was acting under highest authority were generally acknowledged, even by those who supported a severer policy toward the Southern States. The President and nearly all the members of the Cabinet assured him that the published bulletins had been without their knowledge, and cordially strove to soothe his wounded feelings.[58] The genuineness of character, patriotism, and subordination tempered by proper self-respect, which he exhibited, did not diminish the public regard, but rather heightened it. As to the debatable questions of policy involved in his first convention, he proudly left them to the judgment of time.

The breach of friendship between Sherman and Halleck, which was also caused by Mr. Stanton's bulletins, was especially to be regretted. Their early close relations as young officers going "around the Horn" to California have already been mentioned, as well as the warm personal correspondence between them during the Atlanta campaign.[59] He had been grateful also for Halleck's friendly conduct toward him in his period of depression in 1861, and expressed it strongly in a long letter when Atlanta had fallen and he had won his commission as major-general in the regular army. "I confess I owe you all I now enjoy of fame," he said, "for I had allowed myself in 1861 to sink into a perfect 'slough of despond.'" Halleck's friendship and encouragement had put him in the way of recovering from this.[60] But now his faith in human nature was rudely shocked by finding, apparently, this friendly hand joining in the hardest blows at his fame and honor.

In the first of Stanton's bulletins concerning him, Sherman found copied the dispatch from Halleck giving the rumor of Davis's great "plunder," and the hope of the Confederate leaders to "make terms with Sherman or some other commander," by which they would be permitted to escape out of the country with this treasure.[61] The sting of this was in the apparent insinuation that Sherman might be bought. It naturally roused him to explosive wrath. Had Mr. Stanton quoted the final sentence of Halleck's dispatch, it would have shown that the latter intended no such thing. It concluded, "Would it not be well to put Sherman and all other commanding generals on their guard in this respect?"[62] The apparent insinuation was in the Secretary's bulletin by the omission of this sentence from the quoted dispatch. Had Sherman seen the dispatch as Halleck wrote it, he would not have been angered by it.

But on the 28th there appeared in the New York papers another dispatch of Halleck to Stanton, dated the 26th, and saying that his subordinates were ordered "to pay no regard to any truce, or orders of General Sherman suspending hostilities, on the ground that Sherman's agreements could bind his own command and no other."[63] This was upon receipt of a dispatch from Beauregard stating "that a new arrangement had been made with Sherman."[64] In the same dispatch Halleck suggested that orders be telegraphed through General Thomas to General Wilson, at the head of a strong cavalry column in Georgia, to mind no orders of Sherman, but, with other commanders in the Gulf States, to "take measures to intercept the rebel chiefs and their plunder," now estimated, rather indefinitely, at "from six to thirteen millions."

The folly of such publications was egregious, and justified Sherman's sarcasm that if anybody was conniving at Davis's escape, it was the officer who gave them to the public. It was, however, the direction to disregard his new truce, embracing Johnston's troops alone and based on their actual surrender, that stirred anew his indignation. He had made a short inspection tour down the coast after starting his columns northward, and saw the dispatch in newspapers he received at Morehead, May 4th, on his return there by steamer from Savannah. In writing General Grant, he characterized Halleck's action as an insult.[65] Fortunately, he had met at Savannah an officer of General Wilson's staff, Captain L. M. Hosea, who had made an adventurous journey across half Georgia to open communications,[66] and in sending a steamboat up to Augusta with supplies for Wilson, he had hurried Captain Hosea back with such full information as enabled Wilson to observe scrupulously the final convention with Johnston whilst vigorously pushing his efforts to capture Davis. These efforts were successful on the 10th.[67]

Sherman's sense of military honor was violated and shocked by the orders disregarding his truce, which were "cordially approved" by the Secretary of War.[68] Grant suggested that Halleck's action was so connected with Mr. Stanton's orders that it might not seem so bad on fuller information,[69] but Sherman's sense of injury was such that in passing Richmond on the 8th he refused Halleck's offered hospitality, saying that after the dispatch of the 26th of April friendly intercourse was impossible.[70] Halleck's was the "soft answer which turneth away wrath," and it is due to him to remember it. "You have not had during this war, nor have you now, a warmer friend and admirer than myself. If, in carrying out what I knew to be the wishes of the War Department in regard to your armistice, I used language which has given you offence, it was unintentional and I deeply regret it. If fully aware of the circumstances under which I acted, I am certain you would not attribute to me any improper motive. It is my wish to continue to regard and receive you as a personal friend. With this statement I leave the matter in your hands."[71]

But what had occurred seemed to Sherman to be so ingeniously fitted together as parts of a malignant plan, that he replied, "I cannot consent to the renewal of a friendship I had prized so highly till I can see deeper into the diabolical plot than I now do."[72] His words were all the bitter expression of a heart wounded beyond endurance by wrongs which seemed too palpable and plain for discussion or explanation. In the distribution of commands on the peace establishment made soon afterward, Halleck went to the Pacific coast and did not live long. It is to be feared that no opportunity for a full understanding between him and Sherman occurred, though the latter was as placable as he was impetuous; and when he found, as he soon did, that his fame and reputation had not suffered permanent injury, he ignored the past so far, at least, as to show that he harbored no lasting enmity.

Yet Halleck was probably right in saying that he had done nothing but what he deemed his duty, and with no unfriendly purpose toward Sherman. His dispatch of the 26th of April was only one of a series, and it was made to have a different effect, taken by itself, from what it would have had if read in its connection with the others. There is no reasonable doubt that Stanton's angry purpose had been to humiliate Sherman by practically superseding him in command. Halleck knew this and went to Richmond, where he assumed command on the 22d, with full knowledge of the sentiment which then ruled the War Department.[73] In the afternoon of the same day, Grant, on his way to North Carolina, telegraphed him that the truce would be ended as soon as he could reach Raleigh, and ordered him to send Sheridan with the cavalry toward Greensborough, sending also a corps of infantry along as far as Danville.[74] This assumed that by the time these troops could enter Sherman's theatre of operations the truce would have been terminated; for Sheridan was then at Petersburg, and the Sixth Corps at Burke's Station.[75] The cavalry could not be ready to march before the 24th (at the earliest) and did not start in fact till the 25th or 26th.[76] Neither it nor the infantry got beyond Danville or entered North Carolina before they were halted by Grant's order to Halleck of the 26th, received in the morning of the 28th.[77]

No interference with Sherman's truce, either the first or the second, actually occurred. Halleck knew that the first truce would be ended as soon as the two days' notice could expire after Grant reached Raleigh, and long before his troops could come into contact with Johnston's. But he was also moving them by Grant's order, and must not only obey, but must assume that the first truce was no longer in question. It was not necessary or proper for him to explain fully to his subordinates all he knew of Grant's journey and purpose. For their direction it was enough to say they were not to regard the truce which had been made on the 18th and was currently spoken of as "Sherman's truce." Had Sherman known of Grant's order to Halleck and the assumed situation on which it was based, he would not have regarded Halleck's language an insult. Without such knowledge it looked very much like it.

Halleck, however, had to face the question how his subordinates must act if, on coming near the enemy, Johnston should claim a new armistice. He shared the War Department opinion that the negotiation was not sincere on the part of the Confederates, but was a ruse to gain time for Davis's escape with the imaginary "plunder." A pretended armistice is an old and familiar stratagem in warfare. It would seem that Halleck fully believed that Grant would assume actual command, on reaching Sherman (as he had commanded when with Meade during the past campaign), and concluded that any real armistice again made would be in Grant's name. Any other would be a sham or would have been made before Grant was present. Under such circumstances he could not be blamed for telling his subordinates that only Grant's authority or his own must bind them. He was mistaken, in fact, for Grant's arrival was not even known to Johnston, and Sherman concluded the final convention as if Grant had still been in Washington. The curtness of telegrams often creates ambiguities, and when Sherman saw in print Halleck's dispatch of the 26th separated from the rest of the series, he naturally gave to it the meaning which hurt him so. Had he known the rest of the story, he would have seen no treachery to old friendships. The sin was in the unprecedented publications which embroiled everything. In truth, Halleck's order to Meade was more guarded in form than the language of his dispatch to Stanton, for Meade was only told to ignore "any agreements made by General Sherman before the arrival of Lieutenant-General Grant."[78]

A curious theoretic question was raised by Halleck's incidental statement that an armistice by Sherman could only bind his own army. Sherman said he must defend his truce at all hazards till it was duly terminated. Each was right in a sense, but fortunately the laws of war and military regulations would prevent practical difficulty arising. If Sheridan had advanced to Greensborough, Sherman would have met him there, and by virtue of his superior rank would have assumed command and responsibility for the united forces. Besides the orders and instructions from the President he already had, he would have to act in view of any authentic instructions or information which Sheridan might bring. On the other hand, if Halleck had accompanied his own forces, his seniority would have made Sherman his subordinate in the common field of operations; but as commander, he would have to respect, at his own peril, all the rights which Johnston had acquired under the principles of international law. The situation had perplexities only so long as the generals were playing at cross-purposes by reason of imperfect knowledge. Their intelligence and character were such that duty would have been plain to both as soon as they came together.

Stanton made no public explanation of his conduct, but in a conversation with General Howard, he asserted that Sherman's order to his troops announcing the armistice, by saying that when ratified it would "make peace from the Potomac to the Rio Grande," had put the government on the defensive, and made it seem proper to publish reasons for disapproving the terms.[79] This does not touch the question of the wisdom or folly of the matter published, or of its form. Sherman's reason for mentioning the prospect of a general and speedy peace was that the condition of his army under the news of Lincoln's assassination was such that he felt it necessary to soothe his excited soldiery with the hope of soon marching home in triumph, thus turning their thoughts from the vengeance which would have been inevitable if fighting were to be resumed. Instead of appreciating this, Mr. Stanton seems to have jumped to the conclusion that it was an act of vanity or of political ambition which was to be squelched *per fas aut nefas*, and in his passionate and hasty action he compromised the whole administration.

We who were Sherman's subordinates in the field knew so well his integrity and patriotism that we sympathized strongly with his indignation at the appeal to popular sentiment against him. Yet the sense of duty to the country and to the government prevented thoughtful men from being blind partisans of our chief. Without full means of judging of the possible effect of the first convention, if carried out, some of us were disposed to believe that there must have been a mistake on his part, since we were not able to believe that the Secretary of War would publish his "nine reasons" if they had no solid support and were not approved by the President and Cabinet. My personal opinion I wrote in my diary at the time, and I reproduce it to show the contemporaneous sentiment of one who was both a warm supporter of the government and a warm friend of the general. What I have written above will also show how far further investigation and fuller knowledge have modified my judgment. "Friday, April 28th.... Some of the Northern papers are very bitter on Sherman for the terms first offered by him, and it is manifest from the dispatches sent by the Secretary of War to New York to be published there, that the new administration is willing to give Sherman a hard hit. He made a great mistake in offering to Johnston the terms he did, but he has done the country such service that the administration owed it to him to keep the thing from the public and to come kindly to an understanding with him, instead of seeming to seek the opportunity to pitch upon him as if it desired to humble him. In conversation this morning he showed that he felt their conduct very sorely, but I hope he will keep out of controversy with them in regard to it. He complains with justice that they have refused to give any instructions to guide military officers as to the policy to be adopted, and then, when these are forced to act, seem to take pleasure in repudiating what the officers have done, and in humbling them or exposing them to popular odium."

Chapter L

1. Official Records, vol. xlvii. pt. iii. p. 834.
2. Official Records, vol. xlvii. pt. iii. p. 834.
3. *Id.*, pp. 821, 823, 827, 830, 832.
4. *Id.*, p. 833.
5. *Id.*, p. 822.
6. *Ibid.*
7. Official Records, vol. xlvii. pt. iii. p. 824.
8. *Id.*, pp. 263, 264.
9. Official Records, vol. xlvii. pt. iii. pp. 293, 294.
10. Grant to Stanton, *Id.*, p. 293.
11. *Id.*, p. 263.
12. *Id.*, p. 302.
13. *Ibid.*
14. Official Records, vol. xlvii. pt. iii. p. 835.
15. *Ibid.*
16. *Id.*, P. 836.
17. *Id.*, p. 837.
18. Official Records, vol. xlvii. pt. iii. p. 304.
19. *Ibid.*
20. *Id.*, p. 310.
21. *Id.*, p. 309.
22. *Id.*, p. 312.
23. *Id.*, p. 314.
24. Official Records, vol. xlvii. pt. iii. p. 313.
25. *Id.*, p. 311.
26. On April 16th Halleck had been assigned to command the Department of Virginia, thus relieving him of duty as chief of staff of the army in which General Rawlins succeeded him. On April 19th his command was made the Military Division of the James, including besides Virginia such parts of North Carolina as Sherman should not occupy. (Official Records, vol. xlvii. pt, iii. pp. 230, 250.) In reading the Official Records of this period, it must be borne constantly in mind that from two to four days was required to convey dispatches from Sherman to the War Department and *vice versa*,—the longer time in case they were sent by mail, and the shorter when use was made in part of the telegraph lines.
27. Official Records, vol. xlvii. pt. iii. p. 323.

28. *Id.*, pp. 320, 322.

29. *Id.*, p. 321.

30. *Id.*, pp. 350, 355, 482.

31. Schofield's Forty-six Years in the Army, p. 352, etc.; Sherman's Memoirs, vol. ii. pp. 362, 363; Johnston's Narrative, pp. 412-420. General Schofield's recollection is that he wrote the convention of the 26th, Johnston and Sherman being unable to agree: but as it was in substance a transcript of the Grant-Lee terms of April 9th, according to Sherman's note to Johnston of the 24th demanding their acceptance "purely and simply" (Official Records, vol. xlvii. pt. iii. p. 294), the account I have given seems to me best supported by all the evidence.

32. Grant to Halleck, Official Records, vol. xlvii. pt. iii. p. 312; Johnston to York, *Id.*, p. 854; Do. to Governor Brown, *Id.*, p. 855. Sherman's Field Order No. 65, *Id.*, p. 322.

33. *Id.*, pp. 349, 350, 351. 483.

34. *Id.*, p. 320.

35. *Ibid.*

36. *Id.*, p. 322

37. Official Records, vol. xlvii. pt. iii. p. 336.

38. Official Records, vol. xlvii. pt. iii. p. 285.

39. Official Records, vol. xlvii. pt. i. pp. 334, 335.

40. *Ante*, p. 494.

41. Official Records, vol. xlvii. pt. iii. pp. 801, 803, 820, 850; *Id.*, vol. xlix. pt. i. pp. 548, 551, 552, 555; Davis's Rise and Fall, vol. ii. pp. 691, 695; Johnston's Narrative, p. 408; Sherman's Memoirs, vol. ii. p. 373.

42. Official Records, vol. xlvii. pt. iii. p. 482.

43. Dana to Stanton, April 5th: "Judge Campbell and Mr. Meyer had an interview with the President here this morning to consider how Virginia can be brought back to the Union. All they ask is an amnesty and a military convention to cover appearances. Slavery they admit to be defunct," etc. (*Id.*, vol. xlvi. pt. iii. p. 575.) Lincoln to Grant, April 6th, says he had put into Judge Campbell's hands "an informal paper" repeating former propositions and adding "that confiscations shall be remitted to the people of any State which will now promptly and in good faith withdraw its troops and other support from resistance to the government. Judge Campbell thought it not impossible that the rebel legislature of Virginia would do the latter if permitted, and accordingly I addressed a private letter to General Weitzel with permission for Judge Campbell to see it, telling him that if they attempt this, to permit and protect them, unless they attempt something hostile to the United States," etc. (*Id.*, p. 593.) Lincoln to Weitzel, April 6th. (*Id.*, p. 612.) Dana to Stanton, April 7th. (*Id.*, p. 619.) Dana to Stanton, April 8th, with enclosures of papers by Judge Campbell giving the

contents of Mr. Lincoln's written memorandum to him. (*Id.*, pp. 655-657.) When Mr. Lincoln got back to Washington, Lee having surrendered with the Virginia troops and the rebel legislature of Virginia not having assembled or acted, the President withdrew his permission for them to meet, saying he had dealt with them as men "having power de facto" to do what he wished but which was already done. Lincoln to Weitzel, April 12th. (*Id.*, p. 725.)

44. *Ante*, pp. 481, 485.
45. Official Records, vol. xlvi. pt. iii. pp. 656, 657.
46. Gorham's Stanton, vol. ii. p. 235.
47. Official Records, vol. xlvii. pt. iii. p. 266.
48. Nicolay and Hay's "Lincoln," vol. x. pp. 122, 123, 128
49. Official Records, vol. xlvii. pt. iii. pp. 335, 345.
50. *Id.*, pp. 410, 531.
51. *Id.*, vol. xlix. pt. ii. p. 484; vol. xlvii. pt. iii. p. 321.
52. *Id.*, p. 312.
53. Official Records, vol. xlvii. pt. iii. p. 434.
54. *Id.*, p. 445.
55. *Id.*, p. 311.
56. Official Records, vol. xlvii. pt. iii. p. 293.
57. On this subject General E. D. Townsend, as adjutant-general, is a most competent and conclusive witness. (Townsend's Anecdotes of the Civil War, p. 137.) Two little matters occurring at nearly the same time with the Sherman quarrel perfectly illustrate this characteristic in Stanton. General Townsend was in charge of the funeral escort of Lincoln's body, and in New York a photograph was taken of the coffin, in state, in the City Hall, with the drapery of the alcove formed of national flags and crape, with Admiral Davis and General Townsend as guard of honor at head and foot. Stanton read of it in a newspaper, and without further knowledge sent a violent and undignified reprimand to Townsend, ordering him to relieve and send back to Washington the officers on duty, and to seize and destroy the plates. A telegraphic correspondence followed, bringing in the photographers, Henry Ward Beecher, H. J. Raymond, and the military officers, with the proof that there was nothing to find fault with, but rather the desirable preservation of a memento of a memorable scene. There was a retreat, but no apology by the Secretary. (Official Records, vol. xlvi. pt. iii. pp. 952, 965, 966). The other was the permission given the Episcopal clergy in Richmond to continue Divine service in the churches if they omitted the prayer for the Confederate President in their liturgy, that being treated as a demonstration in favor of the insurgent government. General Weitzel was in command, and Mr. Lincoln was in the city when the question first arose whether, in addition to the above prohibition, the clergy should be required to insert, affirmatively, a prayer for the President of the United States. Weitzel supposed

he was acting in accordance with Mr. Lincoln's direction not to be sticklish in little things, stopped at the prohibition, as was generally done by commanders in the field, on the ground that to order a form to be inserted in any liturgy where it did not exist, would be ridiculous for a government based on total separation of church and state. Stanton, hearing of it through Mr. C. A. Dana, informed Weitzel that his action was "strongly condemned," and that he was "unwilling to believe that a general officer of the United States, commanding in Richmond, would consent to such an omission of respect to the President." Weitzel asked whether the direction would apply to Roman Catholics, Hebrews, and other churches having a prescribed liturgy, and Stanton replied *ex cathedra*, in the affirmative, repeating his reprimand. Weitzel now appealed to the President, and the absurd controversy was stopped. Stanton seems to have acted at first in ignorance that individual ministers had no power to insert a prayer into the formal liturgy; but he could not yield when better informed, and a temperate memorial of the local clergy stating the canonical difficulty and their earnest intention to have the change made with all speed possible, is in the Records, "disapproved by order of the Secretary of War"! (*Id.*, pp. 619, 677, 678, 684, 696, 711, 737). Perhaps the nearest historical parallel is Napoleon's order to the Russian clergy to pray for him instead of the Czar in 1812. (Fezensac, Souvenirs Militaires, 4th ed., liv. 2, chap. i. p. 233.)

58. For the correspondence, see Official Records, vol. xlvii. pt. iii. pp. 302, 334, 345, 371, 410, 476, 515, 547, 576, 581, 582, 586, 662; *Id.*, pt. i. p. 40. See also Sherman's Memoirs, vol. ii. p. 375; Conduct of the War, vol. vi. p. 3

59. *Ante*, pp. 174-176.

60. Official Records, vol. xxxviii. pt. v. p. 791.

61. *Id.*, vol. xlvii. pt. iii. p. 286.

62. *Id.*, vol. xlvi. pt. iii. p. 887.

63. *Id.*, p. 953.

64. Official Records, vol. xlvi. pt. iii. p. 953.

65. *Id.*, vol. xlvii. pt. iii. p. 388.

66. *Id.*, p. 371.

67. *Id.*, vol. xlix. pt. i. pp. 515, 526.

68. *Id.*, vol. xlvi. pt. iii. p. 967.

69. Official Records, vol. xlvii. pt. iii. p. 410.

70. *Id.*, p. 435.

71. *Id.*, p. 454.

72. *Ibid.*

73. Official Records, vol. xlvi. pt. iii. p. 891.

74. *Id.*, p. 888.

75. *Id.*, p. 895.

76. *Id.*, pp. 931, 947.

77. *Id.*, pp. 954, 997.
78. Official Records, vol. xlvi. pt. iii. p. 941.
79. *Id.*, vol. xlvii. pt. iii. p. 476.

CHAPTER LI

PAROLING AND DISBANDING JOHNSTON'S ARMY—CLOSING
SCENES OF THE WAR IN NORTH CAROLINA

General Schofield's policy when left in command—Lincoln's Emancipation
Proclamation in force—Davis's line of flight from Charlotte, N.C.—Wade
Hampton's course of conduct—Fate of the cabinet officers—Bragg, Wheeler,
and Cooper—Issuing paroles to Johnston and his army—Greensborough in my
district—Going there with Schofield—Hardee meets and accompanies us—
Comparing memories—We reach Johnston's headquarters—Condition of his
army—Our personal interview with him—The numbers of his troops—His
opinion of Sherman's army—Of the murder of Lincoln—Governor Morehead's
home—The men in gray march homeward—Incident of a flag—The Salisbury
prison site—Treatment of prisoners of war—Local government in the interim—
Union men—Elements of new strife—The negroes—Household service—Wise
dealing with the labor question—No money—Death of manufactures—
Necessity the mother of invention—Uses of adversity—Peace welcomed—Visit
to Greene's battlefield at Guilford-Old-Court-House.

O n Thursday, the 27th of April, the same day on which Sherman issued
his order announcing the final agreement for the surrender of Johnston's
army and the homeward march of most of his own forces, General
Schofield issued his own order declaring "the duty of all to cultivate friendly
relations with the same zeal which has characterized our conduct of the war, that
the blessings of union, peace and material prosperity may be speedily restored to
the entire country."[1] He invited all peaceably disposed persons to return to their
homes and resume their industrial pursuits. He promised also the loan of

captured horses, mules, and wagons to those who had been deprived of their own by the armies, and food for the needy during the period when all must be busy planting if the season were to be made of any avail for agriculture. His order concluded with these words: "It will be left to the judicial department of the government to punish those political leaders who are responsible for secession, rebellion, and civil war with all its horrors. Between the Government of the United States and the people of North Carolina there is peace."[2]

In a separate order of the same date, to remove all doubt as to the end of slavery, he declared that "by virtue of the proclamation of the President of the United States, dated January 1, 1863, all persons in this State heretofore held as slaves are now free, and it is the duty of the army to maintain the freedom of such persons."[3] He recommended immediate fair contracts of hiring and the resumption of profitable industry, so that disorganization of labor might be avoided. He told the freedmen that it was not well for them to congregate about towns or military camps, and that they could not be supported in idleness. All classes of people were thus put upon the footing Sherman had intended in his first convention with Johnston, and Schofield's orders issued whilst Sherman was still with us at Raleigh may be received as an authoritative interpretation of the latter's views.

The Confederate troops were mostly concentrated about Greensborough upon the railroad from Richmond through Danville and Charlotte to Columbia in South Carolina, and the line of railroad we had followed from Goldsborough to Raleigh continued westward to Greensborough. Outposts, Confederate as well as National, remained at stations between the two armies, but no collision had occurred since the truce established on the 19th.[4] Mr. Davis had remained at Charlotte in the interval between the two conventions, but when the separate surrender of Johnston's army was determined, he started southward with a vague purpose of joining some of the smaller organized armies released from the armistice by our administration's rejection of the terms of Sherman's first convention. He tells us that he still hoped that he might cross the Mississippi with such forces as could be concentrated, joining Kirby Smith, who commanded there, and in the last resort carrying a body of irreconcilables out of the country into Mexico.[5] A line of retreat southward had been agreed upon in case Johnston should not surrender, and some accumulations of supplies had been made at Chester, S. C., and other points upon it. General Bragg had been placed in command there, reporting directly to Davis or the Confederate War Department,[6] and some cavalry in West Virginia under General Echols had been ordered to pass by mountain routes to the same region.[7] As soon as the truce was ended by the notice of the 24th, Davis started southward by the route indicated, which kept well to the westward of Columbia by way of Abbeville, aiming to cross the Savannah River above Augusta at the pontoon bridge near the junction of Broad River with the Savannah. His party disintegrated before he entered Georgia, and he was nearly alone with his family when he was captured thirty or forty miles southeast of Macon.

General Wade Hampton was one of those who preferred any alternative rather than surrender, and had opposed even the terms of the first convention to which Davis had assented.[8] He promised that he would bring to Davis's support "many strong arms and brave hearts,—men who will fight to Texas, and who, if forced from that State, will seek refuge in Mexico rather than in the Union."[9] On the 25th, when Johnston's surrender was already resolved upon, Breckinridge sought to arrange that Hampton, with his cavalry, might join Davis,[10] but Sherman insisted on the capitulation of the army as a unit, and Hampton was included. The latter had visited Davis during the first armistice and obtained his permission to bring out the cavalry before the surrender, but on his return to his command, on April 26th, he found that the surrender had been made. Setting up the claim that the arrangement made with Davis had detached his troops from Johnston's army, although they were actually serving in it, he notified Johnston that they and he would not regard themselves as embraced in the capitulation, unless Breckinridge, the Secretary of War, should say they were within it.[11] He had given orders to Wheeler to move the command toward South Carolina, and Butler's division was moving in the same direction.[12] Johnston, feeling that his honor as a commander was involved, sent peremptory orders to Hampton to march back to the position near Hillsborough which he had abandoned. He gave Wheeler similar orders.[13]

Breckinridge gave Hampton the opinion that the troops were bound by the capitulation, though Hampton himself might not be.[14] The latter thereupon informed Butler and Wheeler that he could give them no orders, and asked leave of Johnston to withdraw his former letter, substituting one which only claimed personal exemption from the surrender.[15] In transmitting this, he sent a long letter of apology, explaining his embarrassment. He asserted that in his consultation with Mr. Davis a plan was agreed upon to enable the latter to leave the country. He must now either leave him to his fate or go with him under the ban of outlawry. He thought his personal duty was to go, but would leave his command to abide the terms of the convention, or if any joined him, he said, "they will be stragglers like myself."[16] Enough "straggled" to make up Davis's escort to about 3000 men, comprising six brigade organizations; but Hampton seems to have thought better of the determination to be an outlaw, and though he did not give his parole with the rest of Johnston's command, he did not join Davis.[17] His explicit statement of the aim of Davis's flight warrants us in concluding that the dream of further military operations beyond the Mississippi was never a serious purpose. After the disbanding of the escort at the Savannah River, Breckinridge and Benjamin reached the coast of Florida and escaped to

Cuba. Mallory and Attorney-General Davis seem to have reached their own homes; Reagan remained with his chief, and was captured;[18] Bragg and Wheeler were captured near Athens, in Georgia, using questionable ruses to escape.[19] General Cooper, the adjutant and inspector-general of the Confederate army, remained at Charlotte, and received the benefit of Johnston's capitulation, while he did all in his power to preserve the Confederate archives, which were there in railway cars.[20] This digression to follow the fate of Mr. Davis and the group of civil and military notables who were with him in his southward flight, will help us understand some of the peculiar incidents attending the paroling of Johnston's army at Greensborough. I will now return to events of which I was a witness.

On Sunday, the 30th April, the printed blanks for the paroles were ready, and Brevet Brigadier-General Hartsuff, inspector-general on Schofield's staff, was put in charge of the details of their issue. He went up to Greensborough from Raleigh, accompanied by about a dozen officers detailed from the department and corps staff. It had been intended that he should take with him a guard of a regiment I had selected for the purpose, but at Johnston's request the troops were held back a few days.[21] Schofield had arranged the general scheme of subdividing the State into military districts, of which I was to command the western, whilst Major-General Terry took the central, and Brigadier-Generals Palmer and Hawley retained the coast districts which they already had. In anticipation of the formal order,[22] the detachment to guard the arms and stores which should be received came from my command, and I detailed the One Hundred and Fourth Ohio, a regiment which

Gen. Samuel Cooper, CSA

had won high praise in the review at Raleigh for its splendid form and discipline, and which was an orderly, reliable body of men in battle as on parade. It was ordered to take along also its excellent brass band and drum corps, for I meant to have the duties of a garrison performed in the presence of the Confederates with all the honors.

Sherman had left Raleigh in the evening of Friday (28th), to make a brief tour to Charleston and Savannah, by sea, nominally to inspect that part of his command, but really to pass the time whilst the body of his army was marching to Washington, and to avoid visiting that city in the irritation he felt at his treatment by the Secretary of War.[23] Johnston had arranged, on the 1st of May, to send General Hardee down to Raleigh for personal consultation with Schofield in regard to details of the homeward march of his troops, but the satisfactory arrangement of the supplementary terms made this unnecessary.[24] Schofield determined to go to Greensborough himself, starting early on Tuesday morning (2d), and I was asked to accompany him.[25] We left Raleigh by train at seven o'clock, with the One Hundred and Fourth Ohio as a guard, and at Durham were met by a dispatch from General Hartsuff, saying that the whole Confederate army was "dissolving and raising the devil." I telegraphed for another regiment to follow us, and we went on to Hillsborough. There we met General Hardee, who joined our party, and we went on to Greensborough.[26]

As the train left Hillsborough, we passed through a body of Confederate cavalry, and were within the enemy's lines. I confess it was with a curious, half-uneasy sensation that I thus for the first time found myself on the wrong side of the Confederate outposts without having driven them in by a hostile advance. It was not easy to orient one's self at once with the new condition of things, and it would hardly have been a surprise to find that we had been entrapped by a ruse.

This soon wore off, however, and Hardee made the journey a very agreeable one to us. He had been commandant of cadets at West Point just before the war, and had from the first an "inside" view of the rebellion. His "Tactics," adapted to our army use from the French, had been the authoritative guide of our army drill, and by that means his name had been made very familiar to every officer and man among us. His military career had been among the most distinguished, and he had commanded a corps in front of us during the whole Atlanta campaign. There was therefore no lack of subjects for conversation, and the time ran rapidly away. Hardee was in person and bearing a good type of the brilliant soldier and gentleman. Tall and well formed, his uniform well fitting and almost dandyish, his manner genial and easy, his conversation at once gay and intelligent, it would be hard to find a more attractive companion, or one with whom you would be put more quickly at ease.

Our mission naturally led us into a review of the war, and we asked him what had been his own expectation as to the result, and when he had himself recognized the hopelessness of the contest. "I confess," said he, laughing, "that I was one of the hot Southerners who shared the notion that one man of the South could whip three Yankees; but the first year of the war pretty effectually knocked that nonsense out of us, and, to tell the truth, ever since that time we military men have generally seen that it was only a question how long it would take to wear our army out and destroy it. We have seen that there was no real hope of success, except by some extraordinary accident of fortune, and we have also seen that the politicians would never give up till the army was gone. So we have fought with the knowledge that we were to be sacrificed with the result we see to-day, and none of us could tell who would live to see it. We have continued to do our best, however, and have meant to fight as if we were sure of success."

Amongst many other things, our talk turned upon the Atlanta campaign, and he told some interesting facts in regard to Hood's obstinate holding on at Atlanta when Sherman was executing the movement around the place on the south. It happened that my own division held the pivot point close to the works of the city on the southeast, and Hardee's corps occupied the lines in front of us. He said an old woman had been brought to him who said she had gone to General Cox's headquarters to beg some provisions, and the general had told her she could have none, as the soldiers had not enough for themselves. I had no remembrance of such an incident, and such applications were hardly likely to reach a general officer unless he wished to catechise the person for information's sake; but a laugh was raised at my expense as Hardee in telling the story repeated some profane camp expletives as having added emphasis to the refusal, according to the old woman's account of it. Schofield merrily rallied me on a change of habits of speech when not with my usual associates, and refused to credit my protestation that the story only proved that she had seen some wicked commissary of subsistence. Hardee helped the fun by pretending to think of other proof that the woman was right; but he went on to give the matter real historical interest by telling how he had taken the woman to Hood that he might learn what she said she had seen and heard. On her repeating the expression about our not having rations enough for ourselves, Hood exclaimed, "There, Hardee! It proves that it is just as I told you. Wheeler [his cavalry commander who was on a raid] has broken Sherman's communications; he is short of provisions and is retreating north by the Sandtown road. The troops that have moved from the north of the city have gone that way."

Gen. John Bell Hood, CSA

The Sandtown road was a well-known road going northward from the Chattahoochee River at the place named, which was some miles west of the Chattanooga Railroad. It was a plausible explanation of Sherman's movements as far as they then knew them, but had no better foundation than Hood's own hopes and wishes. Yet, Hardee said, Hood stuck to this view till in our swinging movement to the south, we broke his railway communication with Jonesboro.

Then came his hasty evacuation of Atlanta, the destruction of his stores, the explosion of his ammunition, and the night march to reassemble his army at Lovejoy's station. He confidently believed that the siege was raised till Sherman's army was astride of his principal line of retreat, and it was only by the most desperate exertion that he escaped from utter ruin.

On reaching Greensborough we were at once escorted to General Johnston's headquarters, the One Hundred and Fourth Ohio being ordered to remain near the station till more complete arrangements were made. Our object had been to have force enough to guard the arms and stores against petty pillage or destruction, but not enough to provoke a collision with the larger organizations of the Confederates. Johnston had declined the hospitality of citizens of Greensborough, partly from a motive of delicacy, as I suspect, fearing he might compromise those who would thus be indicated as his friends, though his usual custom was to live under canvas rather than in a house. His tents were pitched in a grove in the outskirts of the town, and he awaited us there. It seemed to us, as we approached, that the little encampment was not quite so regular and trim as our own custom required. The wall tents did not sit quite so squarely upon the ground, and the camp was not laid out with regularity. The general indirectly apologized for some of these things by saying that we could not expect the discipline in his army to be fully maintained when all knew that it was on the eve of being disbanded. Indeed our presence there with a detachment of our own troops was partly the consequence of the tendency to disintegration and the consequent breaking down of discipline which was rapidly going on, of which the dispatch which met us on the way was a warning. We learned that the officers of the staff had for several nights stood guard over their own horses, efforts to steal them having been successful in one or two instances. The general himself was the only one who had been exempt from guard-duty. The soldiers knew that the war was over and that there was in fact no superior power to enforce military subordination. They were anxious to make their way homeward, and fearful that they might be treated as prisoners of war if they remained. A horse or a mule was too valuable a prize not to be a great temptation; they naturally thought that as there was no longer a Confederate States government, the men to whom arrears of pay were due had a right to whatever they could seize, and they were not disposed to distinguish between public and private property. The guards set to protect the commissary stores would wink at the pillage of them or assist in it, and the men were inclined to defy any authority exercised in the name of the Confederacy. They remembered the relentless character of the conscription which put them in the ranks, and were kept together chiefly by the assurance that they should all be promptly paroled and helped on their homeward way. The strongest consideration was perhaps the announcement that the parole would be a necessary protection to them against subsequent arrest. It was a curious fact that the moment the blue-coated sentinels began to pace the "beats" around the warehouses, parks of artillery, etc., the submission of these men to the United States authority was most complete. They were scrupulously respectful in their bearing and language, and the groups of them who gathered about with an earnest sort of interest, would obey the slightest direction of the sentry with a cordiality and alacrity which was in singular contrast with the sort of ostentation of defiance they showed toward their own officers.

I have anticipated a little in order to give some idea of the condition of things in Johnston's army, and will return to our interview with the general himself. He welcomed us with dignity, though there was a little reserve in his courtesy that was naturally due to the gravity of the responsibility and the duty imposed upon him. Hardee, as a subordinate, free from this burden, could afford to give way to a natural *bonhommie*, and the difference of situation emphasized the distinctive traits of the men. Johnston was a smaller man than Hardee, his uniform showed less care for appearances, his manner was quieter, but no one would for a moment fail to see that he was the commander. His quiet tones were clear, his gravity was full of conscious power, and the deference shown him by his subordinates was earnest and respectful.

The preliminary details of our task were soon settled. General Schofield had already promised rations to the Confederate troops whilst awaiting the issue of the certificates of parole, and on their way home; to give them railway transportation as far as railroads were running, and to carry out Sherman's offer to let the Confederate horses and mules be distributed as far as they would go, to assist the men on their way, and in putting in a crop for their families' support as soon as possible. When the necessary business was disposed of, the conversation became more general.

General Schofield inquired what was the number of officers and men to be paroled. Johnston replied that he could hardly be definite as he would like to be: his morning report of "effectives" gave only the men answering to their names with arms in their hands in the line of battle. It would not include stragglers or men detached or on special duty. His last return of effectives showed, as he said, about 16,000 men. Wade Hampton, with much of his cavalry, had refused to come in to Greensborough to be paroled with the rest, and were supposed to be either disbanded or to be making their way southward. Johnston thought the place of these might be made up by the classes not enumerated in the return of effectives, and that there might therefore still be about 16,000 in camp who would present themselves to be paroled. He then added that in this campaign their reports and returns had not been kept up promptly, and that he had relied for practical use upon a summary of the morning reports of "effectives."[27] There could be no question as to his complete frankness and sincerity in this. The inquiry was put to make sure that we had enough printed blanks for the paroles, and it was a matter of mutual interest to get their issue completed with as little delay as possible. The Official Records, moreover, confirm his statement as to the abbreviated returns and the numbers they gave, while making clear their loose inaccuracy.[28] The most important fallacy in the Confederate return of "effectives" was that by giving only the arms-bearing men answering to the roll-call, it omitted the growing large class of stragglers hanging about the camps many of whom might be in line when an engagement occurred.

The number of officers and men actually paroled by us in the Carolinas turned out to be 39,012, which included men in hospitals, some naval officers and sailors, the quartermaster's and other special duty, detachments, etc.[29] Johnston's inspector-general reported on 3d May the number of "final papers" issued to the army proper at 27,749, and the number of men who received their share of the silver distributed on April 28th was 32,174,[30] the difference being in the cavalry, where 5000 men disbanded or went off with Hampton before the paroles were issued. The report of the paroles shows also that the Carolina troops had nearly all vanished during the campaign, the Western troops of Hood's old army making the great bulk of those who stayed with the colors.

Johnston was very warm in his recognition of the soldierly qualities and the wonderful energy and persistence of our army, and the ability of Sherman. Referring to his own plans, he said he had hoped to have time enough to collect a larger force to oppose Sherman, and to give it a more complete and efficient organization. The Confederate government had reckoned upon the almost impassable character of the rivers and swamps to give a respite till spring,—at least they hoped for this. "Indeed," said he, with a smile, "Hardee here" (giving a friendly nod of his head toward his subordinate) "reported the Salkehatchie swamps as absolutely impassable; but when I heard that Sherman had not only started, but was marching through those very swamps at the rate of thirteen miles a day, making corduroy road every foot of the way, I made up my mind there had been no such army since the days of Julius Caesar." Hardee laughingly admitted his mistaken report from Charleston, but justified it by saying that all precedent was against such a march, and that he would still have believed it impossible if he had not seen it done.

All the Confederate officers from Johnston downward were very earnest in impressing upon us their confidence that the army gave up the struggle without bitterness, and that we could rely not only upon their keeping their parole in good faith, but in their anxiety to become again good citizens of the United States in every sense of the word. The assassination of Mr. Lincoln was spoken of, as both an odious crime and an extremely great misfortune to the South, tending to involve the future in gloomy doubt by reason of the probable effect upon Northern public sentiment and upon the policy of Congress and the new administration. Hardee said that for himself he thought he should go abroad for a time, till the heated and exasperated feeling at the North should subside, and then return to his home and his private affairs. I do not remember that Johnston opened his mind on this point, and think he was gravely reticent, scarcely choosing to share with strangers, in our relation to affairs, the deep anxiety he must have felt. Hardee's means were understood to be more ample than most of the Southern officers possessed, and a course that was feasible for him was not so for most of them. The task of winning a mere livelihood was by no means a promising one for men left without a profession and without property, in a country that seemed to be irretrievably ruined.

When we closed the interview, I am very sure that we of the National side had already formed a very high opinion of the personal character of the distinguished officers we had met, and had begun to feel a sincere sympathy with them in their manifest purpose to meet honorably and manfully the demands of the new situation. I recorded at the time my own feeling that I had rarely met a man who was personally more attractive to me than General Johnston. His mode of viewing things was a high one, his thoughts and his expression of them were refined, his conscientious anxiety to do exactly what was right in the circumstances appeared in every word and act, his ability and his natural gift of leadership showed without effort in his whole bearing and conduct.

An incident which occurred at the time General Johnston left Greensborough is striking proof of the scrupulous exactness he was determined to exercise in carrying out the terms of the surrender. He had gone southward as far as Charlotte to superintend the last movement of his forces as a body and the final disbanding, and before parting with the members of his staff learned that one of them had preserved as a relic a little cavalry guidon of silk in the form of a national flag scarce larger than a handkerchief. The general immediately reclaimed it, and afterward sent it back under the provision of the surrender which agreed that all captured flags in the hands of the Confederates should be restored. He apologized for the staff officer, saying that he knew no wrong had been meant and the little flag had been regarded as a trifling but interesting relic; yet he felt that there should be no limitation on their part in carrying out strictly the terms agreed upon. The manner in which all this was done, quite as much as the thing itself, showed the earnestness and sincerity of his purpose to do everything in his power to enforce the spirit as well as the letter of every promise he had made for himself and his army. He had returned to his home at Danville, Va., before he had been able to send to us this flag with another that had been omitted, and his solicitude in regard to it, even in the midst of anxiety in regard to his family, was shown by a note which accompanied the parcel. It ran as follows:—

"DANVILLE, June 5th, 1865.

GENERAL,—I have requested Major Shackford, Provost Marshal of this post, to forward to you a small box containing the color, standard, and guidon which I mentioned to you in Greensborough.

I beg you to explain to Major-General Schofield that they were not in my possession when we were in Greensborough, nor until I reached Charlotte, and that they were not sent to him from that place because I expected to visit Raleigh and there deliver them to him. This visit was prevented by the condition of my family. You may remember that the same cause, as I explained to you orally, prevented my delivering them to you in person.
Most respectfully,
Your ob't serv't,

J. E. JOHNSTON.
MAJOR-GENERAL Cox, (U. S. Army.)"

General Schofield and myself passed the night at the house of ex-Governor Morehead, who had urged us to do so. Our host had been one of the leading Whigs of North Carolina in the *ante-bellum* days, and with his friends and neighbors Gilmer and Graham had opposed secession at the beginning; but with the instinct of politicians, they had striven to lead the current they could not stop when once it had carried them away. The house was a comfortable villa in the Italian style, with a tower overlooking the rolling country for a long distance. The architecture was simple but effective, and the house had evidently been a home of comfort and ease in better times. We were frankly and cordially welcomed, and allowed to see the mixed feelings with which the reassembled family accepted the collapse of the Confederacy. Among the young people was a son of the

John Motley Morehead

governor who had been desperately wounded but had recovered. The rebellion had had their devoted support, but they said, "That is all past now," and seemed eagerly desirous to get into accord with the new order of things. The young man told of his army adventures, and compared notes with us as to camp life in the different armies. We were struck with the strong comparison he made in speaking of his wound. A bullet had entered his mouth and passed out at the back of his neck, and he said it felt, for all the world, as if a city lamppost with its cross-bar had been dragged through his head. I have no doubt this gave as good an idea of the sensation as possible, for I have often heard wounded men speak of the feeling of having received a terrible blow from some big and heavy thing, when hit with a musket-ball. The ladies entertained us with half-gay, half-pathetic stories of the way home-life had run on during the long campaigns, and of the ingenuity they were obliged to use to supply the place of tasteful articles of dress or adornment when the blockade had become stringent, and when each little community was thrown almost wholly upon its own resources. The head of the house discoursed more gravely of the situation of the country at large, and tried to forecast the future. Now that the surrender was made, he was anxious that the army should be disbanded and sent home as soon as possible, for the disposition of the Confederate soldiers to pay their arrears by pillage made him fear that his own farm would be stripped bare before they got away. There is no doubt that there was a good deal of cause for such anxiety, especially for leading men whom the private soldiers were disposed to hold largely responsible for all their woes. It was no slight test of character and good breeding, under such anxieties, for the family to pay delicate and courteous attention to the comfort of their guests, and to keep as far as possible in the background everything that might betray their own troubled feelings.

On Wednesday (3d May) General Schofield returned to Raleigh, leaving me in responsible command of the district.[31] By administering the parole to the troops by companies and regiments, keeping a number of officers at work and using abundant clerical assistance in verifying the copies of rolls, the task had been completed in a couple of days, and General Johnston began to move his men southward. General Cheatham with the Tennessee troops marched across the Great Smoky Mountains, but the others were ordered to rendezvous at West Point in Georgia, which was a central place for all who lived in the Gulf States, from which they could most readily reach their homes. While they remained together they were fed by us, and we furnished rations sufficient to sustain them on the journey. Our ration, too, was quite a different thing from theirs, and the men seemed more affected by this bestowal of unwonted and abundant supplies than by any other incident in the surrender. They said it seemed hardly possible that men who were but yesterday arrayed in deadly hostility to them, could now be supplying their wants so liberally.

Whilst they stayed they seemed never to tire of watching our men on duty and on the various parades. Our guard-mounting was particularly a show affair. From the moment the music struck up on the parade ground, and the detachments for the guard from the different companies began to file out and march into place, there was always a large concourse of the men in gray making a most interested body of spectators. The smart appearance of the men, the rapid inspection of arms, of haversacks and knapsacks, the march in review, the assignment to posts, the final marching off the field, all seemed to give them great enjoyment. They said they had not paid much attention to the formalities which so greatly relieve the drag and labor of military life even in the field, and they were ready with cordial and appreciative praise of the discipline and finish in drill which they saw.

As the Confederate troops left Greensborough, I concentrated my own corps there,[32] sending one of the infantry divisions to Salisbury, and Kilpatrick's cavalry division to posts still farther toward the southwest. A visit of inspection which I made to Salisbury gave me the opportunity of examining the site of the recent prison camp there. The treatment of our prisoners by the Confederate authorities is a repellent subject, and I would gladly pass it by and say nothing discordant with the tone of high honor and respectful good-will which marked the conduct of the leading officers of the Confederate forces in the field. We may fairly admit that the resources of the Confederacy had been so taxed that food and clothing were hard to procure, and that their armies in the field were ill-fed and in rags. There is, however, a limit beyond which a government calling itself civilized may not go, and as the public opinion of the world, crystallized into what we call international law, will not permit the wholesale decapitation of prisoners, as might be done by a king of Ashantee or Dahomey, so it forbids the herding of captive men in a mere corral, leaving them utterly without shelter of any sort through the sleet and rain of winter, near the North Carolina mountains. It forbids starving them to death or leaving them to rot with scurvy because they are not supplied with wholesome food and medicines. It is the plain duty of a

The Confederate prison at Salisbury.

civilized government to parole and send home military prisoners who cannot be fed or sheltered. If controversies as to exchange existed, such conduct would have been the surest way to shame us out of any position that was wrong, and the public opinion of the world would have been powerful in making it the more profitable way, as it was the only one not utterly barbarous. I speak with a solemn sense of the obligation to avoid every railing accusation when I say that it would have been humane and civilized in the comparison, if the prisoners at Andersonville and Salisbury had been shot down by fusillades or quickly poisoned by wholesale (as Napoleon was accused of doing at Jaffa) instead of subjecting them to death by starvation and exposure which swept them away at a rate no plague ever rivalled or approached. I have seen too much of the Southern people, in arms in the field and in their homes, to believe for one moment that they would knowingly approve the treatment our prisoners received. But their own reputation before the world makes it their duty to fix the responsibility for a great crime upon those whose commands or whose criminal negligence caused horrors which are among the most odious things in the world's history.

I had seen at Wilmington and Goldsborough the condition of train-loads of these released captives. Their situation has been surgically and medically recorded in the surgeon-general's official reports. There is no room for dispute. They were men reduced to idiocy and to the verge of the grave by the direct effects of hunger and exposure and the diseases necessarily connected with such suffering. They were not of the dregs of humanity, who might be said to fall into animality when the restraints of society and of discipline were removed. They were many of them men who had respected positions and refined surroundings at home. These were the victims who looked vacantly with glazed eyes and could mumble no intelligent response when asked their names, where was their home, what was the name of the mother that bore them.

At Salisbury the pen in which part of the prisoners had been kept was still to be seen. There were, as I remember it, two levels or "benches" in it, and in the little bluff or slope from one to the other were still to be seen the holes the poor prisoners had dug to make a little cave in the earth that would drain itself and give some shelter from the winter weather. I talked to women of the place who with tears upon their faces told of the efforts some of them had made to have the worst of the treatment corrected, or to procure some mitigation of the want and hardship. The evidence seemed conclusive that any marks of common sympathy or Christian pity were repelled by the officials in charge of the prisoners and treated as indications of disloyalty to the Confederate government.

The Confederacy was full of places where the almost limitless forest afforded timber without end, and the labor of the prisoners themselves under the same guards that garrisoned the prison would have comfortably housed and warmed them, and then the scant and wretched rations would not so soon have been the cause of emaciation and disease. The risk of escape would not have been great, and I doubt if as many would have got away as in fact managed to do so in the actual circumstances. The almost certainty of sickness and death nerved many a man to incredible exertions to be free, who would have waited more patiently for an exchange if his condition had been less intolerable or less sure of a fatal result. But even if there had been some more escapes, it would be no argument in favor of the horrible system which was adopted. There is no resemblance between the situation of prisoners in a pen, and that of soldiers in bivouac. The latter build shelters of rails or of brushwood, if they have no shelter-tents, and they are very rarely stinted in firewood. Their active life helps to preserve their vigor. To liken these to men without shelter of any kind and without fire enough to cook by, herded inside a ring-fence in winter weather, is an abuse of words. Enough of the shocking subject!

As soon as headquarters baggage could be brought up I established my own camp in the northern edge of Greensborough, in a grove which was part of the grounds attached to the mansion of Mr. Dick, since that time judge of the United States District Court. The first impression of the people was that all government was now in the hands of the army, and we had no little difficulty in correcting it. The policy of the government was to recognize the ordinary courts and local magistrates, and to support their authority in preserving the peace, punishing crimes, and determining ordinary civil rights. The political organization of the State was left subject to such changes or conditions of reconstruction as might be prescribed by national statute. The army, however, was the present palpable fact. The muskets and the cannon were physical engines of power that everybody could see, and everybody knew that the commandants of department and district could use them if need be. There was, therefore, a national tendency, both in civil magistrates and in the people, to refer all sorts of questions to the military authorities. I tried in good faith to make it understood within my own district that we were averse to meddling with local affairs, and wished the ordinary current of civil administration to run on in its accustomed channels till it should be replaced by that which should have the new authority of a reconstructed state under Acts of Congress. I not only promulgated this through the military channels, but I accepted several invitations to address the people at different points and explain our attitude and purpose during the interregnum, and to give them serious advice as to their conduct in the very trying circumstances in which they were. It need hardly be said that the gist of this advice was to recognize the absolute death of the system of slavery, to deal with the freedmen with perfect sincerity as free laborers who were at liberty to make the best bargain they could for their labor, and to confine for the present their political activity to the duty of keeping alive such local magistracies as would prevent the community from falling into anarchy. There was a wistful solicitude noticeable in people of all classes to know what was to become of

them. Their leaders had educated them to believe that the success of the National
arms would mean the loss of every liberty and subjection to every form of
hateful tyranny. Yet they almost universally showed a spirit of complete
resignation to what might come, and a wish to conform obediently to everything
enjoined by the officers of the occupying army. It was the rarest thing in the
world to meet with anything like sullen resistance or hostile or unfriendly
utterances.[33] My own stay in North Carolina did not extend into the period of the
provisional governments authorized by Acts of Congress, and I was not
personally witness to the varying phases of sentiment among the people at that
time.

The political character of North Carolina during the war had been
different from that of the Gulf States. We found very few indeed who were
known as "original Secessionists." The "old Whigs" had given the tone to public
sentiment, and the community as a whole had sincerely desired that the Union
might be preserved. Yet a society based upon slavery had such community of
interest with the States further south that it was soon dragged into the secession
vortex. When once war had begun, the growth of hostility against what was
regarded as their public enemy was rapid, and in every State a war party in time
of war has a great advantage over the opposition. The charge of "giving aid and
comfort to the enemy" is too powerful a weapon against the minority, and the
outward appearance was soon that of almost complete unanimity in the desperate
struggle to make secession a success. Party leaders were borne along upon the
current, and vied with each other in extravagant professions of devotion to the
Confederacy.

In such circumstances the men who were at heart opposed to the war
thought they were doing all that was wise or prudent in making what they called
a constitutional opposition to the Davis government, professing to acquiesce in
the Confederate organization, but urging the negotiation of peace on the best
attainable terms. In the fever of actual conflict the following of such men was
small, although it seemed plain to me that a majority of the people of the State
sympathized with them at heart.

The outspoken Union men were, almost as a matter of course, treated as
traitors, and lived under a reign of terror. In the mountains, where their numbers
were considerable, they were the victims of a relentless guerilla warfare, as the
same class was upon the other slope of the Great Smokies in East Tennessee.

Out of these classes came the elements of new struggles for political
power. The minority naturally felt that their time had now come, and were not
altogether patient with the principles of our democratic Constitution, which
require that a majority shall not be disfranchised, and which therefore make it
practically impossible that a minority shall rule. At the time I am speaking of,
these elements were quiet in the first stunning effect of the collapse of the

Confederacy; but we could see the tendencies to antagonisms that were to agitate the State during the next decade.

The negroes were, of course, of none of these parties. Very few of the whites were in favor of emancipation on principle, though all accepted it as the inevitable result of the war. Tacitly or avowedly, they all admitted that the fate of the "system" had been the real issue at stake, and that the surrender meant universal freedom. But the colored people were ignorant, and had cherished strange illusions as to the change which was to come to them. It was a common belief among them that the whites were to be stripped of all property, and the land to be given to them. We had heard curious discussions among them around the camp-fires, in which they had apportioned the real and personal property among themselves. The faith that they were each to have "forty acres and a mule" was of a little later growth. The first noticeable thing among them after the surrender was the almost universal disposition to quit work. It would have been very natural that they should wish for a great holiday, and try to realize their freedom by extending it at their own will, and thus prove to themselves that no man was their master. But in addition to this, they seemed to fear that any continuance of the relation of laborers for their former masters would cover some waiver of their right to freedom. Yet, as they had hopes that the real estate would be given to them by the National government, they were disinclined to leave the old home. The outcome was that for a time they occupied their old quarters and asserted a kind of proprietorship in them, whilst they "struck" from labor.

When it is remembered that the kitchen of Southern houses is a detached building of which the servants have exclusive occupation, it will easily be understood that the situation was anything but comfortable for housekeepers. Oftentimes they could neither hire cooks nor get access to the open kitchen fire and the rude utensils which the colored people appropriated as their own. According to my observation, the Southern white women were very systematic and thorough in the supervision of household work, but were necessarily ignorant of the actual manipulation. They knew what flour and other ingredients to weigh out for a batch of bread, but they had never done the baking. Some of them tried their first experiments over the open fire with "Dutch ovens" and other primitive implements, whilst a group of colored women sat around commenting drolly but most exasperatingly upon the results. As a temporary compromise, we were obliged to "clear the kitchen" by military authority, making it known that that was part of the "house," and that if the mistresses of the mansion had to do their own work, it was not necessary that it should be done before such an "audience." Such a social crisis is always short, but it is very severe. No doubt those who have gone through it look back upon it as one does upon the day after a fire, when the wretchedness of dirt and destruction seems hopeless, but, like other mundane things, soon passes away and is spoken of as all "part of a lifetime."

A delicate and amiable lady, whose fortune at her marriage had been of that ample sort which was measured in Southern parlance as "a hundred negroes," herself told me, with a mixture of tearful pathos and recognition of the comic side of it, of her own first efforts to make a batch of soda biscuit for her husband and children after she got possession of her kitchen. She knew all about the rule, but in new practice the rule didn't work. The ingredients got wrongly mixed; the fire was too hot or not hot enough; some biscuits were burnt to a crisp, some were not cooked, and none were eatable, and her heart was ready to break at the prospect of her family's condition till something could be done to remedy the trouble. In more than one household our officers' messes helped tide over the painful interval by giving camp hospitality and friendly assistance to their new neighbors. We frequently heard housekeepers say that if they only had the snug ranges of Northern kitchens within the house they would have made light of the labor; but their outdoor kitchens and primitive methods, which produced appetizing results in the hands of colored cooks who had been brought up to them, were killing upon those who had been delicately reared.

We saw more of the domestic form of this social anarchy than of farm labor, for the outdoor work could wait, whereas the indoor work could not. The same difficulty was everywhere, however, and the intelligence of the community soon hit upon temporary expedients. Such men as Mr. Gilmer and Judge Dick took the lead in advising the colored people to avoid their apprehended risk of compromising their freedom, by hiring out temporarily to work for others than their old masters. By thus changing about, the consciousness of working under a voluntary contract was stronger, and the uneducated brain was less puzzled to tell whether any change of situation had really come. We did our best to dispel the notion that wealth and idleness were to follow emancipation, and to encourage the freedmen to resume industrious labor as the foundation of real freedom and independence.[34] The peaceful character of the colored people was shown even in what they supposed was a great revolution in their favor. There was no rioting or angry disturbance,—no effort to accomplish anything by force. They abandoned for the time their usual employments, and congregated in their quarters or in groups about the streets, waiting for some great thing to happen. There was, of course, plenty of talk and some excitement, but even this gradually diminished; and as they began to realize that without work there would be no food, they made such bargains as suited them, and the affairs of the plantation and of the house began to move on. The owners of property did not hope for profits; they expressed themselves earnestly as anxious only that such crops might be raised as would save the community, white and black alike, from absolute destitution. I know of prominent examples of well-known men offering the farm hands all that they could raise for that season if they would only go to work and plant something which could still ripen into food. The season was advancing, and a little delay was very dangerous. The last chance for a crop in that year would soon be gone. The influence and advice of sagacious and prudent men was never more useful, for society seemed to be resolved into its original elements when all authority but the military went for nothing. As soldiers, we refrained from meddling in civil affairs, but it was understood that we should preserve the peace and allow no force to be used by others. It was a time when everybody felt the need of being patient and conciliatory, and the natural authority of known character and wisdom asserted itself. Everybody soon went to work to make a living, and the burning problems of political and social importance were postponed.

A serious inconvenience was immediately felt in the lack of a circulating medium. The Confederate currency was at once made worthless by the failure of the rebellion, and there was nothing to take its place. The extent to which its depreciation had gone was amusingly shown by a printed notice and list of prices I found posted in a country tavern, already some months old. In it the price of a dinner was put at ten dollars, and other meals and accommodation in proportion. Still this currency had served for business purposes, and it being gone, the community had to go back for the time to primitive barter.

We had opportunity to notice to what great straits the people had been reduced for two years in the matter of manufactured goods of all kinds. Factories of every sort were scarce in the South when the war began, and resources of every kind were so absorbed in the war that there was no chance for new ones to spring up. Carriages, wagons, and farm implements went to decay, or could only be rudely patched up by the rough mechanics of the plantation. The stringent blockade shut out foreign goods, and the people were generally clothed in homespun. In many houses the floors were bare because the carpets had been cut up to make blankets for the soldiers. Ladies made their own shoes of such materials as they could find. They braided their own hats. They showed a wonderful ingenuity in supplying from native products the place of all the articles of use which had formerly been imported from foreign lands or from the North. Taste asserted itself, perhaps all the more in such discouraging circumstances, and feminine refinement and love of adornment worked marvels out of the slenderest materials. A home-made straw hat ornamented with feathers of barnyard fowls and domestic birds was often as jaunty and as pretty as any Parisian bonnet. Simple dyes were made to give to coarse cotton stuffs a lively contrast or harmony of pure colors as effective as the varied and elaborate fabrics from the European looms. In some respects this self-dependence heightened the personal advantages of those who excelled in ingenuity, in taste, and in skill; for the clothes indicated better the character of the wearer than those which are made on one pattern in the shop of a fashionable mantua-maker.

Adversity has such uses and such compensations that I should hardly reckon the poverty of the Southern States during 1864-65 as a burden greatly felt in private life. All such things are comparative, and where all the people undergo the same privations, the odious comparisons and jealousies between richer and poorer disappear in a measure. A simple life full of great enthusiasms is one a philosopher may find much satisfaction in, and has, many a time, been pictured as an ideal calculated to bring out the best qualities of men and women and therefore to make life more truly enjoyable. I greatly doubt if Southern people, in looking back on the war time, find anything to regret in the simple fare and plain dress of the enforced economy of that period. The real griefs and burdens, if I am not mistaken, came from other sources. Among thoughtful people there must have been from the summer of 1863 serious doubts of the possibility of a successful outcome of their struggle, and a growing and unhappy conviction that the fearful waste of life and treasure would be in vain. They must have had grave misgivings also as to the righteousness of a cause which championed an institution condemned by the whole world and in conflict with the general progress of Christendom. To see their best and bravest consumed in the fire of successive battles, and to be waiting only till the slaughter should make it impossible to keep armies in the field, must have been a grief and a suffering which made all physical deprivations seem small indeed.

I think I cannot be mistaken in the judgment I formed at the time, that to the great body of the Southern people it was a relief that the struggle was really over; that they breathed more freely and felt that a new lease of life came with peace. They had been half conscious for a good while that it must end so, and they were in the mood to be at least resigned, if not readily to profess the pious conviction that "it was all for the best." With the reactions and political exasperations that came later, I have here nothing to do. My purpose has been to reproduce, as far as my memory serves, the scenes and the surroundings of that last military duty of the great war. Why it was that the mellowness of spirit which seemed then so prevalent could not have ripened without interruption or check into a quicker and more complete fraternization, belongs to another field of inquiry. The military chronicler stops where he was mustered out.

A summer ride which a party of us took to the battlefield of "Guilford-Old-Court-House" may be worth noting as an encouragement to believe that our descriptions of the scenes of our own engagements need not become unintelligible even in the distant future. Among the combats of our Revolutionary War, Guilford Court House ranks high in importance; for the check there given to the invading British army under Lord Cornwallis by the Continental forces under General Greene was the turning-point in a campaign. Greensborough is the present county-seat of Guilford County, and the "Old Court House," a few miles distant, has disappeared as a village, a few buildings almost unused being the only mark of the old town. Natural topography, however, does not change its material features easily, and in this case a cleared field or two where the forest had formerly extended seemed to be the only change that had occurred in the past century. With General Greene's official report of the battle in our hands, we could trace with complete accuracy every movement of the advancing enemy and his own dispositions to receive the attack. We could see the reasons for the movements on both sides, and how the undulations of surface and the cover of woods and fences were taken advantage of by either commander. Military principles being the same in all times, we found ourselves criticising the movements as if they had occurred on one of our own recent battlefields. It brought the older and the later war into almost startling nearness, and made us realize, as perhaps nothing else could have done, how the future visitor will trace the movements in which we have had a part; and when we have been dust for centuries, will follow the path of our battalions from hill to hill, from stream to stream, from the border of a wood to the open ground where the bloody conflict was hand to hand, and will comment upon the history we have made. It pointed the lesson that what is accurate in our reports and narratives will be recognized by the intelligent critic, and that the face of the country itself will be an unalterable record which will go far to expose the true reasons of things,—to show what statements are consistent with the physical conditions under which a battle was fought, and what, if any, are warped to hide a repulse or to claim a false success. Nature herself will thus prove the strongest ally of truth.

END NOTE.—General Cox was the spontaneous choice of the "Union Party" of Ohio for Governor, and was nominated at its Convention held in Columbus, June 21,1865, while he was still engaged in his military duties in North Carolina. At a ratification meeting, held in the evening after the Convention, Senator Sherman said, speaking of the ticket: "It is headed by a gentleman who is not only a soldier, but a statesman and scholar,—a man of the highest and purest character,—a man who, in all the walks of life, will be a model for us all. I thank you for that nomination,—although I believe the people made it before the Convention met." At a reception in honor of General Sherman given in Columbus, July 13, 1865, the general himself was called on to speak. After mentioning Grant, whose fame was secure, and McPherson, his beloved companion in arms, he said: "And here is General Cox, who is your candidate for Governor,—a man who did his whole duty from first to last and did it well and will do it to the end."

General Cox was elected by a handsome majority, served one term, returned to the practice of the law, and in 1869 was appointed Secretary of the Interior, by General Grant. Retiring to private life at the end of twenty months, he occupied many positions of trust and honor: President of the Toledo and Wabash Railroad, Member of Congress from the Toledo District, President of the Cincinnati University, Dean of the Cincinnati Law School, etc. His reading was extensive; his scholarship profound. In microscopic research he attained world-wide distinction and he received the Gold Medal of Honor at the Antwerp Exposition of 1891, for excellence in micro-photography.

He was thrice honored with the degree of LL.D., the last time by Yale College, in June, 1877. As an indication of the esteem in which he was held by those among whom he went as an armed invader, it should be mentioned that one of the degrees was conferred by the University of North Carolina, in June, 1870.

He was a member of the American Philosophical Society, the Massachusetts Historical Society, the Royal Microscopical Society, the American Association for the Advancement of Science, the Military Historical Society of Massachusetts, the Cobden Club, and a number of others.

His contributions to the magazines, historical, literary, and scientific, were numerous, and his series of critical and biographical reviews in "The Nation," from the beginning of its publication to the summer of 1900, constitutes a most valuable and interesting commentary on public men and affairs and military operations at home and abroad.

His public addresses, many of which were published in pamphlet form, were marked for their literary finish, their wealth of learning and suggestion, their deep philosophical insight, and their lofty patriotism.

He had little leisure for writing books, but has contributed to the literature of the war several articles in "Battles and Leaders of the Civil War"; the volumes on "Atlanta," and "The March to the Sea, Franklin and Nashville," in the Scribner War Series; "The Second Battle of Bull Run," in which he took issue with the findings of the Second Court of Inquiry in the Fitz-John Porter case; "Franklin," a detailed account of that battle, together with the events leading up to it and the controversies following it; the last half of Force's "Sherman" in the Great Commander Series; and the above "Military Reminiscences." However much men may differ with his conclusions, none who knew him personally ever questioned his candor and sincerity, and his disposition to be absolutely fair in his treatment of others.

Chapter LI

---

1. Official Records, vol. xlvii. pt. iii. 330.
2. Official Records, vol. xlvii. pt. iii. p. 330.

3. *Id.*, p. 331.

4. *Id.*, p. 250.

5. Davis, Rise and Fall, vol. ii. pp. 694, 696.

6. Official Records, vol. xlvii. pt. iii. p. 836.

7. *Id.*, p. 795.

8. *Id.*, vol. xlvii. pt. iii. p. 813.

9. *Id.*, p. 814.

10. Official Records, vol. xlvii. pt. iii. p. 837.

11. *Id.*, p. 841.

12. *Id.*, pp. 841,847.

13. *Id.*, pp. 844, 846. See also Johnston to Sherman, *Id.*, p. 336.

14. *Id.*, p. 851.

15. *Id.*, pp. 845, 847.

16. Official Records, vol. xlvii. pt. iii. p. 846.

17. Davis, Rise and Fall, vol. ii. pp. 689, 690.

18. *Id.*, pp. 694, 695.

19. Official Records, vol. xlix. pt. i. pp. 550, 551.

20. *Id.*, vol. xlvii. pt. iii. pp. 842, 848.

21. Official Records, vol. xlvii. pt. iii. pp. 349, 351, 483.

22. *Id.*, p. 396.

23. *Id.*, pp. 337, 338.

24. *Id.*, pp. 366, 857.

25. *Id.*, p. 376.

26. Official Records, vol. xlvii. pt. iii. p. 376.

27. See pp. 424, 425, *ante*.

28. Official Records, vol. xlvii. pt. ii. p. 1382; pt. i. p. 1059; pt. iii. p. 839.

29. *Id.*, pt. i. p. 1066.

30. *Id.*, pt. iii. pp. 850, 867.

31. Official Records, vol. xlvii. pt. iii. pp. 394, 407.

32. Official Records, vol. xlvii. pt. iii. pp. 376, 384, 396, 502.

33. The same disposition in the people was noticed elsewhere in the South. Halleck said, in a dispatch of April 22d, "From all I can learn, Richmond is to-day more loyal than Washington or Baltimore." (Official Records, vol. xlvi. pt. iii. p. 888.) Sherman sent similar reports from Savannah. (*Id.*, vol. xlvii. pt. iii. p. 371.)

34. See General Schofield's Order No. 46; Official Records, vol. xlvii. pt. iii. p. 503.

APPENDIX

• RECOMMENDATION FOR CORPS COMMAND

"HEADQUARTERS DEPARTMENT OF NORTH CAROLINA, WILMINGTON, N. C., February 24, 1865.

LIEUT.-GEN. U. S. GRANT, Commanding Armies of the United States. City Point, Va.

GENERAL,—I respectfully request that the troops in this department which do not belong to the Twenty-third Army Corps may be organized into an army corps, and that Maj.-Gen. Alfred H. Terry be assigned to its command. Also that Maj.-Gen. J. D. Cox may be assigned to the command of the Twenty-third Army Corps.

I am, General, very respectfully, your obedient servant,

J. M. SCHOFIELD, Major-General."[1]

([*Letter of same date.*])

"... I have asked for the assignment of General Cox and General Terry to corps commands, both because the strength of my command renders it desirable, and because it will enable me to leave either the one or the other in command of the column which I may not be with at any time."[2]

"HEADQUARTERS, ARMY OF THE OHIO, GOLDSBOROUGH, N. C., March 22, 1865.

LIEUTENANT-GENERAL GRANT, City Point, Va.

Near a month ago I wrote you a letter requesting that Maj.-Gen. J. D. Cox be assigned to the command of the Twenty-third Army Corps, and that the remaining troops in this department be organized into a corps in command of Maj.-Gen. A. H. Terry. Having received no reply, I presume that my letter did not reach you; therefore I beg leave to renew the request. But if it be not deemed advisable to organize a corps for General Terry, I nevertheless respectfully request that Major-General Cox may be assigned to the command of the Twenty-third Corps.

J. M. SCHOFIELD, Major-General."

• **Endorsements of Cox's Promotion**

"GOLDSBOROUGH, N. C., March 23, 1865.

I approve this. I know that General Cox is a good officer, and General Terry has the best possible reputation. General Schofield will want two corps organizations as soon as possible.

W. T. SHERMAN,

Major-General, Commanding."[3]

"CITY POINT, VA., March 25, 1865.

HON. E. M. STANTON, Secretary of War, Washington.

General Schofield recommends and I approve the appointment of General Cox to the command of the Twenty-third Corps. He also asks the organization of the balance of the troops in his department into a corps under General Terry. This will be of great advantage to his command. I would suggest that Terry's corps be called the Tenth.

U. S. GRANT,

Lieutenant-General."[4]

• **The orders promoting Jacob D. Cox to Major General**

"GENERAL ORDERS No. 49.

WAR DEP'T, ADJ'T-GENERAL'S OFFICE, WASHINGTON, March 27, 1865.

By direction of the President, the following assignments are hereby made:

I. Maj.-Gen. A. A. Humphreys, to the command of the Second Army Corps.

II. Maj.-Gen. J. G. Parke to the command of the Ninth Army Corps.

III. Maj.-Gen. J. D. Cox to the command of the Twenty-third Army Corps.

IV. All other troops in North Carolina not belonging to corps in General Sherman's army will constitute the Tenth Army Corps, of which Maj.-Gen. A. H. Terry is assigned to the command.

By command of the Secretary of War,(E. D. TOWNSEND,(Assistant Adjutant-General."[5]

Appendix

1. Official Records, vol. xlvii. pt. ii. p. 559.
2. *Ibid.*
3. Official Records, vol. xlvii. pt. ii. pp. 960, 961.
4. *Id.*, pt. iii. p 18.
5. Official Records, vol. xlvii. pt. iii. p. 34.

If you liked this book, you might try these!

Rebel Gibraltar
by James L. Walker, Jr.

One Good Man: Rev. John Lamb Prichard's life of faith, service and sacrifice
by Rev. J.D. Hufham; edited by Jack E. Fryar, Jr.

Derelicts
by James Sprunt

The Story of Brunswick Town & Fort Anderson
by Franda D. Pedlow & Jack E. Fryar, Jr.

The Battles for Fort Fisher
by Jack E. Fryar, Jr.

www.dramtreebooks.com

www.ingramcontent.com/pod-product-compliance
Lightning Source LLC
Chambersburg PA
CBHW072004060426
42446CB00042B/1828